T0374208

The Turning Point

HARRY BLUE

authorHOUSE®

AuthorHouse™
1663 Liberty Drive
Bloomington, IN 47403
www.authorhouse.com
Phone: 1 (800) 839-8640

© 2018 Harry Blue. All rights reserved.

No part of this book may be reproduced, stored in a retrieval system, or
transmitted by any means without the written permission of the author.

Published by AuthorHouse 05/31/2019

ISBN: 978-1-5462-2356-6 (sc)
ISBN: 978-1-5462-2355-9 (e)

Print information available on the last page.

Any people depicted in stock imagery provided by Getty Images are models,
and such images are being used for illustrative purposes only.
Certain stock imagery © Getty Images.

This book is printed on acid-free paper.

Because of the dynamic nature of the Internet, any web addresses or
links contained in this book may have changed since publication and
may no longer be valid. The views expressed in this work are solely those
of the author and do not necessarily reflect the views of the publisher,
and the publisher hereby disclaims any responsibility for them.

CONTENTS

CHAPTER 1

I Was Born in L.A. California

I was born in Los Angeles, California, in 1955. Life wasn't easy for the six of us as far as I can remember. It was 1959, and I was about four years old. My brother was in grade school; he was five. Mama was about eight months pregnant and about to deliver the fourth child of the bunch. Her nephew was there; he regularly came to check on her, and on this day, I was glad he did.

My brother had come home from school with a painting, and it was that time of the day to take a nap. Mama always made sure of that. We went to the room as we were told, but as kids, we played around till we got tired. But on this day, we did just the opposite. There was one thing left to do before sleep, and the painting played a big part. We were playing with it when, all of a sudden, my brother told me to go into the kitchen, look in the cabinet, and get some matches, which I did.

When I returned to the room, we start playing again, and this time, he lit the painting. Now we were trying to put it out and couldn't, and the flame caught the bed. Again, I'm glad my cousin was there, because I took off running, screaming, and hollering, leaving my brother in there to fight the fire. I told Mama the business, and my cousin got busy. He ran out and came back in with a big, black water hose and put out the fire.

But it was not over. Pops came home from work and got the news, and we knew it was on. He wore a one-inch-wide black belt, very thin. My brother was first. He took him into the bathroom. I heard some loud talking and then some hollering, and I knew I was next. But they only stayed there a short time, and as he came out crying and rubbing, I started crying after looking at him. I went in, but something strange happened—Pops didn't spend half the time on me. I wondered why, but I didn't ask, just left well enough alone. But I still wanted to know why.

I walked out and went to the room, and my brother and I looked at each other. Then we crawled into the bed and did what we were told—we went straight to sleep.

My mother was an old-fashioned woman. When we were born, she used a dresser drawer for our bed. Yeah, we were very poor, and she made do with what we had.

Finally, it was six of us, and we moved to a new place in 1962. I started school at this time. There were eight of us living in a one-bedroom house. Pops was a drinker—a heavy drinker—and he was a very jealous man. Mama was scared of him, but you wouldn't know it, because that's how strong she was. He would leave in the early part of the day and come back at three or four in the morning. This time, I was in bed with Mama.

There was a crash, and a four-by-four piece of wood came through the window, scaring the hell out of us. The lights were still off, the front door open, and now we all were awake. We heard his voice, and he was drunk. Mama was in the kitchen trying to cut the lights on, but Pops met her, and there were some scissors hanging on the wall that Mama always kept there. Everybody knew where the scissors were if needed. They both bumped heads, and he reached up, put his hands on the scissors, and, with the lights still off, came down with them. I believe he was trying to kill her because if she had not put her hands up and blocked them, he would have. But she was thinking, and she was on top of it, knowing what he was trying to do. He hit her in the palm of her hand. It was deep enough for stitches, but she was the doctor; she knew best.

Pops had a good heart, but he could be dirty. I remember one occasion after the two of them had split up but were still seeing each other. At that time, they had an acquaintance named Jack. He had a dog, a German shepherd, named Jack as well. This one night, she and Pops went somewhere down the line, and something must have happened between them because she left him and starting walking home by herself. As she was walking, a cabbie pulled up beside her and asked if she needed a ride. Pops spotted her talking to the cabbie, so he jumped out of his car and started walking toward her. He opened the door and tried to put her in his car, but she refused. Jack the dog came out of the bushes barking. The cab driver looked up and freaked out, jumping back in his damn car. He saw the odds were against him, so Mama walked home.

The next morning, I went to the door and looked out to see the dog asleep on the porch. That's how I knew Mama was telling the truth. Mama had written the cab number on a piece of paper and put it on top of the window sill in the bathroom. As Pops walked in, the number must have fallen into the bathtub. He saw it, picked it up, and called her in. He had a Mum deodorant jar that was flat and fit in the palm of your hand. They don't make them anymore. When she walked in, he grabbed her by her hair, threw her in the bathtub, and beat her bloody bad in the head until he got tired. My younger sister grabbed his leg, hollering and crying. I guess he thought he had better quit while he was ahead. We were standing there before him crying our little heads off, and there was nothing we could do. Mama was bleeding like a stuck pig. My brother and I got towels and wiped the blood from her face as she sat helplessly. But she was a strong lady, and God was there again.

I always wondered why he was trying to kill her. My mother took care of us as best she could. She wrote the Lord's Prayer on a piece of cardboard and nailed it on the back door for us to read. As the six of us sat on the floor, she read it to us. My brother and I learned to read, and one of us would read it every night before bed.

The answer I was looking for finally arrived. There was one born before me, and after Pops went into the army, I came into the world, fathered by another man. I never said she was a saint. She did what she did, but she carried herself as a woman. Now I see why there was so much friction when I was in their presence. The day President John F. Kennedy was assassinated in 1963, Pops came in the house after being out all night. He put on a two-piece navy blue suit, walked out of the house, and didn't even look back to say bye or anything, and he was never seen again. Really, that was the best thing that could have happened to the family, and we were all glad.

Later on down the line, Mama met this dude through a friend of hers, but there was something about him I didn't like either, but there was nothing I could do about it. I thought Jack was going to be her friend, but that didn't happen; instead, she fell for another guy. Everything was all right for awhile, but then shit started to change. Mama wasn't a drinker, but she started. After that, things started to unravel; it was his way or no way. If something she did wasn't right, he'd start hollering at her. After everybody got drunk, he liked to show up and show out, thinking he couldn't be touched, even though Mama had a few male friends she could call upon when needed. He always thought somebody was after her, and he couldn't stand it.

We're still staying at the same place. "Brother Number Four" and I were playing in the yard, and there was a car out there, so we decided to play on it to see who could jump the farthest. I jumped, and he jumped, but he jumped one too many, and his foot got caught on the tail of the car, and he tripped and fell on his head. I went running to Mama, telling her what happened. She came out to check him out. His head looked to be swollen. We thought he was going to the hospital, but Mama wasn't having it. A maintenance man who worked around the houses took a liking to my brother. I don't know if he felt sorry about his head or what, but he built him a coaster using some Union 5 skates. It was the best on the block, and he was proud of it.

CHAPTER 2

Move Into A Bigger House

The house started to close in on us, and it was time for us to move. We had to get something bigger, so we moved around the corner in 1964. It was a three-bedroom. A lot of people's lives were starting to change. At the age of nine, I had a lot of friends. We were in the backyard shooting marbles. We also sold blue chip stamp books for $1.25 a book. This came in handy because $0.10 was hard to come by, but things were cheap at that time. Mama used to send one of us to the store to get her a pack of cigarettes. They were $0.26 a pack. She smoked Winston Red hundreds. A bottle of RC Cola cost $0.14, and gasoline was $0.26 a gallon. Things were very cheap then. We stayed next door to the landlord. He was a pretty good old dude. He took a liking to Mama and Pops, and he was getting sick to the point where he couldn't take care of his self, so he told Mama and Pops that he'd let us stay in his house, paying no rent if we took care of him. Before we moved Mama and Pops start going to Las Vegas with some of the neighbors and leaving us at the house. On this night, we were alone doing things we weren't supposed to do. My brother again was jumping off the bunk bed, and his foot got hung again. This time his chin hit the bunk, and he bit a hole straight through his tongue. He had a heavy foot for some reason, and it always kept him in trouble. It's was an all-night thing. There were no adults around, and we couldn't go outside because we were told not to. We were so scared we didn't know what to do but nurse his wound and cry, hoping Mama would come home soon. His mouth was in bad shape. Finally, the next day, the front door opened early. We were so glad to see her, we gave her a hug and told her what had happened. She was glad to see us too but mad because she was always there when we woke up in the mornings. Doctor Mama went to work. She got some hydrogen peroxide and made him drink it. A couple of days went by before he started to eat; then things went back to normal.

The time came for us to move in next door. The first time I walked into this house, it was the spookiest place I had ever seen. There was a long hallway, four bedrooms, and one bathroom. The house was old. I had never seen so many fleas in my life. As you walked across the front yard to the door, you felt a bite and looked down, and there'd be a million of them on each pant leg. There were so many in the backyard too. There was a garden there, as well as four bird dogs and pigeons in a cage. The fleas killed them all. After a while, the landlord got so far gone that he died. When he did, so did those damn fleas.

The year 1965 rolled in. I was ten years old now, and I'd seen a couple of deaths in my young life. The second happened when this guy walked up onto the porch, knocked, and asked for Pops. He wasn't there. As he stepped off the porch, he tripped. There was a piece of steel sticking up from the ground about 3 inches high. His head hit it and died right on the spot. That was the first time I'd ever seen someone die before my eyes. You know, it's funny—when he died, immediately flies surrounded his mouth. I didn't know at that time that flies were associated with death. Really, it was something to see.

Mama met this lady that lived down the street with a handful of kids and a husband. They became the best of friends. Finally, I found out why I was a mama's boy. Mama told her, "If something should ever happen to me, please take care of my second son."

"Why," she asked.

"My firstborn's father went to the army for two years. I met this man, and he was born before he got back. When he did get back, I had the other four."

Now things were starting to make sense, and I knew why he was jumping on her so much.

She was a nice lady. She had about nine kids, and there were six of us. She turned out to be my godmother. Over the years she turned out to be my second mama. Those two were just alike. Boy, would they feed you. A person could get a plate with no questions. I spent nights over there and woke up among piss and bedbugs just to keep from sleeping in that spooky-ass house. Yeah, that buddy of mine used to *piss, piss, piss.*

Bikes were the thing in those days. Some families didn't have money, so we stole what we wanted. I had a bucket that didn't look worth a damn, but Mama didn't have any money, so I had to make do.

It was 1965. I had just turned ten, and the Watts riots had begun. The people tore Watts up. Folks went in and out of stores and took everything that wasn't nailed down. Supermarkets, banks, jewelry stores, and pawn shops—you name it—they were all hit, not only in Watts but across the whole city. The city burned for seven days and seven nights. People were running out of stores with half a cow, half a pig, whatever you could put your hands on. There was this radio station with a disc jockey named Wolfman Jack, a white boy. As the city burned, you could hear him say, "Burn, baby, burn."

Finally, the National Guard came in to quell the riots. I was walking in the area of the activity with a straw hat on and carrying a few bike parts. The National Guard told everybody to get off the streets by 3:00 p.m. or there would be consequences, so the streets were cleared. The looting was over, but the suffering continued. There were no streetlights, and there was no food. The stores were all empty, and there was very little gas. It might have seemed fun at the time, but we were all living off of each other, so we all paid the price. To this day, my sister remains prepared for a disaster: she has a generator, bottled water, canned goods, even tents.

The riots left thirty-four dead and more than a thousand injured. The relationship between police and African American community was strained. The Civil Rights Act had passed in 1964, but some states tried to get around the new law; the ghetto conditions of Watts were deplorable. But things got really bad when a white highway patrol officer pulled over a black man for suspicion of drunk driving. After he failed the sobriety test, the driver became angry and began resisting arrest in front of one or two hundred onlookers. The police assaulted the driver, and things escalated from there. It was sad, but we, the people, got through it.

An incident happened one night at about eight o'clock. We were standing on the porch, and there, in the air, was a single-engine plane, coming down nose first, headed for the projects. It went in through the roof of one of the buildings. Miraculously, as if by the grace of God, it didn't explode. I told a couple of my buddies, "Let's go check it out," so we ran down and climbed the wall to the roof. The scene was frightening. Somebody said real loud, "It's going to blow!" so we climbed down, but it didn't explode. It took until midmorning the next day before they came from the roof with the plane. The pilot he was in one piece, but he was broken up. That was a sight to see, something that will never leave me.

CHAPTER 3

It Was An Old House

The house was starting to fall apart. When it rained, water poured through the roof. There were leaks in every room. The ceiling was falling down. I mean the whole inside was a mess: pots filled with water in every room—there was not even a pot to cook in. There was another house next door, available in the back. The landlord lived in the front. When he saw how we were living, he let us move in. It was three bedrooms for $75.00 a month. How happy we were then. What a relief! We were now living in three houses in a row, all right next to each other. We stayed there for about a year. Pops and the landlord couldn't get along, so we had to move again. Pops ran across a piece of land with two houses on it, one in the front and one in the back. We took the house in the back, figuring we could rent the one in the front to help pay for both houses. Pops had nothing but old-school cars at the time: a 1954 and 1955 Cadillac, 1958, 1959, and 1962 Ford, a 1960 Buick Roadmaster, and in 1959 Pontiac. I can go on and on. He was a mechanic. That's how he came across cars.

Mama had started to drink heavily now, and Pops had

begun to get heavy-handed with her. He just kept jumping on her. We saw that things weren't looking so good for the home team, with all this fighting going on again, but there was nothing we could do about it.

A lady and her little family moved into the front house, and she and Mama became friends and drinking buddies. They didn't last long, maybe six months. They didn't want to pay rent, so Pops gave them the boot.

Pops had a cousin. Everybody called him Cuz. He had seven girls and one boy by an Indian woman. He was a good guy, but he was a damn fool too, always chewing Double Mint gum. He had nice-looking white teeth, and he professed not to smoke or drink. However, he did drink three S Tonic, an iron supplement with 12 percent alcohol content. He would turn up the bottle, and when it came down the bottle would be empty. He would also take these pills that we called red devils. Like Valium, they get you all high and sleepy. He'd often be so high he could hardly walk. He's dead now. He was crossing the street when a car hit him.

He used to keep a .25 semi-automatic pistol on him. One evening, Cuz was together with this dude who lived across the street which was Pop's friend. He gave him the gun to hold for him. Somehow Pops found out. He went right over to him to get it, but it wasn't happening. The dude said, "No," and before you know it they were wrestling over the gun. The dude outweighed Pops by a hundred pounds, so he overpowered him and kept the gun. He took off running down the street, pointing the gun at Pops. I told Pops to duck. As he did, the Pop ran between the fence and the house, getting away. Later that night, at about 3:00 a.m., we heard someone knocking on the back door. It was Pops. I opened the door, and there he stood with a 12-gauge single-barreled shotgun. He came in and we talked for a minute, and then we went to bed. In the morning, Pops went to talk to the dude to get the gun back, but he didn't want to give it up, so they started arguing again. The dude told Pops to call his mama and tell her, "Her little son becoming home in a pine box."

Pops told me to go through the front house, to the back house, get the gun, and bring it to the front door, placing it around the corner. "The next time he says anything else about my mama, I'm going to shoot him in the ass," he said. And so he did. The next time the neighbor mouthed off, Pops walked right onto the porch, reached in, got the shotgun, and shot him in the ass. He hollered like a newborn calf. The only thing that saved him was a wooden plank.

Pops laughed. "I told you to keep my mama's name out of your damn mouth." The man's wife, nine months pregnant, came outside, cussing at Pops. Pops put another shell in the gun. The next door neighbor was Pops' hunting buddy. He came out as well after hearing the shot to see what was going on. Pops was aiming the gun at the man and his wife, but his buddy, seeing what was happening, knocked the gun toward the air. It went off.

Just then, Cuz pulled up in his car. It was a 1957 yellow Chevy station wagon. Mama was in the car. Pops jumped in the car, wanting to leave immediately to go to another state. As soon as they left, the police pulled up. They started asking questions. When they came to me, they asked me what happened, and I said I didn't know anything because I didn't want to say the wrong thing. I just kept my mouth shut. Mama was in the car with Pops, and I didn't want to see her hurt. They stayed away for a couple of hours, but eventually, they came back. They had talked Pops out of leaving. Later that day, the dude made it home from the hospital. Cuz went over to his house and they talk things over. He gave him the gun back and agreed not to press any charges. They just left well enough alone and became buddies again.

One thing I know for sure: Pops was a very overprotective man, and very jealous of Mama. He would hurt you badly when it came to her and her kids. He was stupid jealous. I was his favorite, and he never knew that I was his little enemy because of the way he was treating my mama.

I transferred to a new junior high school. The district I was in was kind of scary, but when I went to school my brother always looked out for me. We used to go to this hamburger stand, the name of it was Pappy's. The hamburgers were only $0.20 each, and they were delicious. We would visit the place going to and from school. Every time, a couple of dudes would try to take our pennies. My brother wasn't having any of it. He would always get into a fight. I would tell him, "Let's just go," but he wasn't having any of it. Finally, they got the message and left us alone. The hamburger stand was across the street from Watts Towers. It had been built years earlier, way before my time, from 1921 to 1954. (Yes, it took thirty-three years to complete the construction.) It was made of glass, a small piece of concrete, and all other types of small objects. It still stands today.

CHAPTER 4

Did A Lot Of Rabbit Hunting

Pops loved to hunt. He always wanted me to go with him so I could chase down the rabbits. He would give me a .38 with a single bullet in it. I guess he didn't trust me. At the end of the day, I had packed up about seventy-two rabbits. However, before we left, I shot and killed a bobcat. That was a scary moment. This time, Pops let me carry a 4-10 bolt-action shotgun that held three shotgun shells. As the cat came running at me, I hit it with a single shot, but all it did was slow him down. Pops' friend, seeing it running toward me, said, "Shoot it again!" I hit him with two more shots. That laid his ass down. He curled up into a ball and died. Boy, you couldn't tell me anything that day. I'd had the best shot of the day at age 13.

The plan now is to save the hide, but it didn't work out. After we got home, they dug a hole and put him in the ground. I thought they knew what they were doing and that we could pull him out eventually, but they let him stay in the ground too long, and all that was left was nothing but hair. If I knew then what I know now, I would have nailed him up on a board. He would have come out just right.

The time came for us to move again. We had moved more than the law allowed, but we had to do what we had to do. There was an empty three-bedroom house back in the hood. Rent was cheap at $65.00 a month. Mama was getting welfare, about $300.00 every two weeks, plus a bunch of food stamps every month. There was a neighborhood store about four or five houses away, and we needed money, so my buddies and I decided to break in one night. We knocked a hole in the wall, went in, and came out with about twenty cases of Colt 45. That's what Mama and Pops used to drink. We had no place to take it, so we asked if we could put it in the house. Mama said yeah, it was right up her alley because that was her drink. After that, there was beer all around. We drank some, sold some, and give some away.

We were broke but never hungry. Mama kept a pot of something on the stove, so we always had something to eat. Even if she didn't know you, she would feed you until you were full. She rented a ringer-type washing machine for $2.50 for the weekend, and we washed clothes from Friday to Sunday. Mama wouldn't let us go anywhere until we finished. One day, my sister was helping out. She wasn't paying enough attention as she put a piece of clothing through the ringer, and her arm got caught. She hollered and cried until my brother and I got her arm out. Thankfully she turned out all right.

Everybody thought Mama was cool and hated when Pops jumped on her. My brother and I were getting older now, and all this was about to change. One day, Pops and his hunting buddy came to the house. They were all drinking, and he told me to do something. I said no, and we exchanged words. I thought he was going to put his hands on me, so I turned the tables. I hit him first, in the face, knocking him down, then stomped on him and kicked him in the mouth real good. Suddenly I felt someone pulling me off him. It was Pops' buddy, laughing and telling me to stop. I stopped, and he said I should come with him for a few days. Pops had this murderous look in his eye, so it was safer that way. His friend was laughing so hard because you never seen anyone ruff that ass before. I think Pops was surprised too from the look on his face. Two or three days past, and he decided to take me home, hoping everything had died down. When we got to the house, I walked in through the side door. As I sat down on my bed, I looked up to see a 12-gauge shotgun pointed at my face. Pops told me I had better never put my hands on him again. I said okay, scared to death, crying and slinging snot out of my nose. I knew he wasn't joking. That was over with for the time being, but it wouldn't be long before something else got Pops to pop off again.

There was still beer left, about ten cases, so there were still a few dollars to be made. There was a pool hall and the liquor store, built right next to each other in the hood, and a junkyard across the street, so shit was going on all day, every day in LA. The liquor store opened at 6:00 a.m. and closed at 2:00 a.m., so you could get just about anything you wanted at any time. I was still a youngster at the time, trying to understand life. Pops had been with us now about five years.

My brother played in the orchestra at school, the clarinet. When you left grade school, heading to junior high, you went to the auditorium first for your introduction to a new life. They played a record for you, "Mercy, Mercy,

Mercy," an old-school jam that you'll never forget once you've heard it.

Not having much in life you learn to deal with it, to the point where I didn't care anymore what people said about us. We were poor but proud. I was playing the clarinet as well. I used to sit in the front row and play, wearing combat boots that were way too big for me. People would see me and laugh, but I continued to wear them as if they were Stacy Adams and play on. When I got to the new school, it was a lot different. I thought it was so cool being with the big boys. It was a Crip game. Their leader's name was Big T. It was 1968, and he had a hell of a crew. They ran a big part of South Central and were very dangerous. They all wore coveralls and looked like bodybuilders. They were huge. That's how I found out about the Crips and Bloods. When they bumped heads on the school campus, there was a slight uproar, but nothing too serious.

I met a girl and we got close. Each day during the school week, Mama would give me $0.50 for lunch. Instead, I would save it until Friday, leaving me with $2.50. I would head over to Watts, over to this girl's house. I would sit and talk with her and bought her soda and chips—whatever she wanted. Man, I thought, I was Mr. Big. In the eighth grade, $2.50 was a lot of money.

On the weekend, Pops and Mama had it going on. Usually, it was one of Pops' friends, who would come to play the guitar. They would start on Friday and go on until Sunday night. It was a house full of drunks, drinking and having fun. Females would be there too, singing the blues. After all the men and women (who were old enough to be my mamma and daddy) fell asleep around me, my brother and I would go into their pockets and purses. Yeah, we knew it was wrong, but we had needs too.

The only thing I hated about the Boom-Boom Room was that somebody always started some shit. It would last for two or three days, and there would often be some gunplay as well. I was afraid for Mama and my brothers and sisters. The gun thing was right up Pops' alley. He was always the protector, trying to look out for someone else's ass. Like I said, he was a jealous man. He's lying and waiting, playing dead, hoping to catch someone talking to Mama so that he could act like a damn fool. Depending on the situation, he might jump on both of them, thinking that she might want to be with whoever was talking to her. Now, I'm not saying my mama was a saint, but when my friend and I came around, we would all be out walking to school.

I was in the seventh grade and had just moved to my new school. My brother was there, so I followed him. I knew things were going to be okay if we missed the occasional class. But time would go by so fast, before you knew it, half the day was gone. Maybe we go back after lunch, but soon it became the same thing every day: we would ditch the whole day, drinking and hiding from the police, hoping we didn't see mama or somebody who knew her. If Mama caught us, we knew the consequences would be severe. Mama's friends wouldn't take wooden nickels either; there was no Child Protective Services at the time, so the mothers had to look out for each other. They knew when we were lying. When Mama got on our butt, you needed Jesus, because she'd stay on it for a *long* time.

Pops did mechanic work and kept me under a car with him. It was okay for a while, but it got old. The money was slow, and you were always dirty. My little girlfriend would sit and wait for me until I got done. Half the time she was hungry, and I wouldn't get my money until late in the day, so I had to change it up and find another trade. There was a junkyard across the street from the liquor store. At about ten o'clock one night, a couple of guys and I jumped the fence. Copper, brass, car radiators, diesel radiators—that's what we were after. That's where the money was. We did two or three times a week, and we didn't care about the police. Most of us were under sixteen and, hell, $150.00 three or four times a week, each, was a lot of money in your pocket back then. Finally, I got a chance to buy me a pair of Levi's and shoes, things I'd never had because mama couldn't afford it.

After hanging out with the older guys, you started picking up on things, and I did—trust me—some good and some bad. I was in and out of school now, doing pretty much what I wanted to. It was 1968, and I was fourteen years old. I had met this girl, and we were trying to mix it up. She was a couple of years older than I was, and she had a big family, and they love to fight, I mean really mix it up. This girl I was messing with was pretty cool, but she also stayed in Watts. I was on the west side of town now, but I walked every day to see her. Her mama and step-daddy were gone for work, so it was just me, her sisters, and a couple of brothers hanging around the house until it was time for me to go back to my place before school was out. I had a buddy that was messing with one of the sisters.

We moved again, this time to the tough side of the city. The Hoover Crips ran that side of town. The move meant that I had to change schools. As I was checking in, I saw a crew of dudes in jumpsuits. I'll be damned if it wasn't Big

T and his boys, walking the campus like they owned it. They were built pretty well and looked ready for anything to jump off.

Later in my life, the gang scene would affect my life in a way I could never imagine.

CHAPTER 5

Ditching School

Friday came around, and I made my move. I told Mama, but she already knew I wasn't coming home, because it was the weekend. I told her I was spending the night at one of the fellows'. If she wanted me, she could put her finger on me, because everybody knew us. It was getting to the point now, to where my girlfriend and one of her sisters wanted to get out of the house, but they had to be in by ten o'clock night. One night we went past curfew, and we had nowhere to go, so my partner and I took the girls around to the pool hall, where everybody was hanging out, standing beside the barrel for heat.

My buddy and I jumped the fence to make some money. The dogs they had weren't worth a red nickel; they were more scared of us than we were of them. One of our buddies had a car, so we got what we were looking for and got the hell out of there. In total, we loaded up about eight diesel radiators. We took them over to my house, put them in the backyard, covered them up, and then went and got the sisters. The five of us stayed out all night. We had a blanket for the females so it wasn't too cold for them. We had to stay with the money so we wouldn't come up short. Yeah, we had some onlookers waiting to catch us slipping.

Daylight hit, so we loaded up and went to a junkyard to sell the items. They paid better than $85.00 for a radiator. Now we were winning. Everyone was happy. Now we could eat. On the way back, we thought about what we should do first. First, we needed to get these women out of our hair, so we did. The Authorities (their mama and daddy) had gone to work, so now we could move around and do our thing. We went into the house and got fresh. I gave my girl a few dollars and gave Mama a few pennies too. Couldn't leave her without. She told me, "Don't get in the doghouse, because I can't come and get you out."

"Okay," I said on the way out the door.

This girl I was dealing with was starting to come around quite a bit. Mama was the kind of person who didn't like other women in the kitchen, and she definitely didn't want us sleeping in the same bed, but where there's a will, there's a way. When everyone went to sleep, I would sneak into her house.

We had to move again, so back to the hood we went. There was an empty house back in the hood, and it was the same old thing, no change—everyone back at the Boom-Boom Room once Friday night rolled around. Pops would start jumping off his thing by getting his friend RC to play the guitar. When he'd play, people would show up. He had a speech disability, and you couldn't understand a word he was saying, but the man could sing his ass off. Funny, huh? God gives talent to people like him. He never thought he could make it because of his disability.

I remember being at the pool hall with the fellows,

hanging out and shooting dice. I was looking for a fade, and there was an old guy in the game. I kept hollering "Bet!" so he opened his mouth and replied, "Bet!" You young muthafucka, I got more money than you and your mama on the county." I was drinking a short dog, which was a bottle of Thunderbird wine. When he said that, I slapped him right upside his head with a bottle repeatedly.

His granddaughter begged me, "Mister, mister, please, please don't hit him anymore, please!"

I said, "You better get this old bird before it is slow walking and sad music."

After he left, the police drove up, got out of the car, looked down at the blood on the ground, which looked like jelly, and for some reason came straight up to me, asking me questions about the blood. I had no answer. I looked down and saw that there was quite a bit of blood there. I felt bad for the old dude and hoped he was all right. A couple of days later, I saw the dude. He saw me but acted as if he had never seen me before. I never asked any questions. I just left well enough alone. This was a hustling corner. Everybody had some kind of hustle going on, from aluminum cans to panhandling, robbery, selling dope, fighting, maybe killing.

On Monday, Pops left. He was gone a while, so Mama visited an old friend who lived down the street. He was about eighty years old, and they were drinking buddies. The old man could drink. His choice of drink was Foster's, Old Taylor, and that Gordon's gin, 100 proof. Two or three hours later Pops came home—no Mama, no food, and he didn't know where she was. Finally, she hit the door, then she hit the floor. He slapped her down, calling her whore and bitch. He always thought Mama was with a man. Like I said, he was a jealous dude. My brother and I looked at each other, trying to figure out how to stop him before he killed her. We had to be on point. We had only one shot at his ass. Once he came home full of his drink, pissed off mad, it didn't take too much to set him off. His understanding was zero, and the fool would turn into a beast. One night he had a stick in his hand when he walked in. He said something to mama, and she didn't have the right answer, so he hit her again, and if she hadn't put her hands up he would have knocked her right in the face. As it was, he broke her arm, and she came back from the hospital with a cast.

Once we were old enough, a couple of buddies and I sat in the house, in the dark, waiting for Pops to come in. As soon as he stepped his ass in the house, we were going to get some fat off that head. He never came home that night. I guess he knew what time it was. As time went on, he was back at the house more, sometimes he would jump on mama and we wouldn't know it.

One day, down at the pool hall, it was some old-school, down-on-the-ground dice shooting. Pops was there and was down to his last five. He needed a fad. Something happened, and Pops lost, but he said the other dude cheated, so he took his money and walked out. Pop left and came back later with a shotgun and jacked the whole game, but he only picked up $5.00, which was the amount of money he was cheated out of. He was a hot mess.

This family that I know had a lot of brothers and sisters, and they all went for bad, no joke. Just like every weekend they were shooting at each other behind trees, knocking off the bark. Pops even had two stepdaughters. Just like our stepsisters they were from state of Texas. The oldest one had cats running behind her as if she were the beast of the queens if you know what I mean. These fools loved gunplay. There was this one dude who she settled down with and married. It was three of them, two staying in LA and the other dude was from Oakland CA living with his parents.

I was about fifteen years old when Pops' friend died. He and his buddies wanted to drive up to Oakland, but they all started drinking, I mean that hard Thunderbird wine. Pops drank whiskey; wine got him drunk too fast. Anyway, they needed somebody to drive, as they planned to drink along the way. I had just learned how to drive and had never driven on the freeway. This was about an eight-hour drive, but Pops encouraged me, so I said okay. One of them started the trip and continued for about two and half hours. When he was ready to get to the bottle, they put me behind the wheel. Man, that was a scary thing, but after about an hour I got comfortable, so I stayed focused and took it in.

I learned how to drive when my brother and I went hunting awhile back with Pops and one of his buddies. We were riding in a 1958 Chevy station wagon—manual transmission, three speed in the collar. I could never get it into second gear, so I messed up the transmission, leaving us stranded a hundred miles from the house. Pops and his buddy hitchhiked back to get some help, leaving us there until they got back. It seemed like forever. It was cold as hell, with about fifteen funky dead jackrabbits. They were mad too, and they were dead. After about five hours, they made it back.

After we got there, I said, "Thank you, Lord." If I hadn't taken the wheel, we wouldn't have made it that day. After settling in, we went to the funeral home to see his mother.

As we were walking through the establishment, we walked into a room containing twenty to thirty caskets. As we walked and talked, looking for her, I was petrified. I'd never seen this many dead folks in my life. After he found his mother, we headed back to the house. The next day, after we woke up, one of the sons found his daddy dead in his bed. That threw me for a loop. "Damn," I said, "that's a hell of a blow, but there's nothing you can do about it."

After the funeral, it was time to get back down south before they drank up all the gas money. I was thinking about the drive back home, hoping that somebody would take the first turn, because four hundred miles is a long drive for a sixteen-year-old. One of the others did take the wheel, knowing that the Grapevine was not a highway to be played with. It was a two-hour turnpike at a 4,500-foot elevation. You were between mountains, up high in the canyon, and if you were not on your game, everybody was going to die.

Finally, we made it to LA, and I was glad to see the sign welcoming our arrival. Now I can get back to my program and make some money because my pocket was flat. That night the boys and I got together and made our way over to the fence. It would be the last time. The Lord shut me down. A radiator fell in my foot—a big one, a diesel radiator, about two hundred pounds. I couldn't walk. My leg and foot started to swell. In 1971, Mama took me to a clinic for an examination. I was admitted with a fever of 104, and they couldn't get it down. They called the children's hospital, and the next thing we knew, I was in an ambulance. I was admitted to emergency. Seeing the fluid in my leg, they stuck a needle in my knee. I broke it in there. They took me to surgery right then. When I woke up the next day, I was in bed with an IV in my leg, wrapped up pretty tight. They had me in isolation due to the infection.

A month passed, my temperature still hadn't gone down, and my leg was dangerously swollen. Mama came up to sign some papers sending me back to surgery. When I saw her, I couldn't believe it. She was dragging her feet, her mouth all twisted. I assumed she had been drinking. Later, when I found out what was really happening, I started crying. Turns out she hadn't been drinking at all. She'd had a stroke.

CHAPTER 6

In The Hospital When Earthquake Hit

After two months my fever was still high. They made an incision about 6 inches long on the side of my leg and inserted two tubes to drain the excess fluid.

Finally, my girlfriend came to visit. She was now seven months pregnant and getting bigger all the time. She took the bus to see me, two hours each way. When she stayed, they gave her a couple of blankets and a pillow to make her as comfortable as possible. I think they didn't want to be responsible if anything happened. It was nice to have somebody there to keep your mind off things besides the walls.

The fourth month I was there, I was on the sixth floor one morning. It was about 5:00 a.m. when suddenly the room started to shake. The bed rolled from side to side. I thought that maybe a helicopter was dropping off or picking up some patients, but that wasn't the case. It was an earthquake, longer than any I had been in before. With a magnitude of 6.5, the San Fernando Earthquake took down the hospital on February 29, 1971. Thankfully, the area I was staying in didn't fall. I remember one hospital that fell in Slymar, resulting in large loss of life.

On March 12, 1971, I became a father of a baby girl at the age of sixteen, still in my hospital room, with a fever that hadn't broken. The IV was in me the whole time. At this point, they were getting pretty close to cutting my leg off. Doctor Miller was a pretty cool guy. He spoke to me about my ordeal and how things should turn out. He picked me up and sat me down on the couch, then pulled out a pack of cigarettes and asked if I wanted one. (Yeah, you could do that at the time.)

"Yeah," I said. As we smoked, he spoke about the operation and what needed to be done. The infection I had was on the bone. They need to remove it, which meant scraping down the bone.

The day of my operation, I was scared. I remember them putting me out, and when I woke up, I saw my girlfriend standing by the bed. That's all I remember from that evening because I was out again. The next time I woke up, doctors and nurses were standing all around me. I listened as they explained the outcome of my procedure. It was good news. My temperature was going down. A couple of days went by, and they had to change the bandage. I got to see the work they had done. The wound was about eighteen inches long left wide open to the bone to let it drain.

My brother and a couple of buddies came by to holler at me. He told me that Mama wasn't doing so well. I kind of knew that already, because I could see it in his eyes. There was another woman around the corner that Pops was messing with. I think he thought Mama was going to die and was preparing himself. I went to church, I ask God to look after Mama and my brothers and sisters. I still had an IV in me at the time, attached to a bottle. I had so much pain that they had to put me to sleep to change the bandage, and they kept me in isolation because of my open wound.

Six months passed, and the doctor came into the room to give me the rundown. The fever was finally gone, but I had to go home in a body cast because it wouldn't take much to snap the bone. When they took off the brace, I looked at the leg.

"Damn!" I said.

It was so thin that it scared me. The first time I stood up I got hot and dizzy. The cast was getting heavier and heavier by the moment. It must've weighed forty pounds. I had to learn how to walk again, as well as go to the restroom and do other things.

When I got back to the hood, it was such a sense of relief to see my front yard full of familiar faces waiting to see me. Finally, I got a chance to see my child. She was beautiful. She was my queen. I was only a kid myself, but I knew right away that she needed to eat, and that meant I need to get back on my feet.

The day finally came when I got the cast-off. Man, what a relief. I stayed in the hospital about three days to learn how to walk again, and they gave me a lot of therapy. I was weak in my legs but determined to get back on my feet because of my little girl. I went home on crutches. It was 1972 now, and I was doing pretty well. It took me a year to walk normally again. I still had a bit of a limp, but I was up to 90 percent strength. My girlfriend told me she was going to have another baby. I was okay with this, but I was only seventeen at the time. I wasn't really worried, though, because my girl's mother took care of her, and she lived with us, which meant my mother took care of all of us.

CHAPTER 7

Getting On My Feet After 18 Months

It was 1972. I was walking much better now, and I was looking for another way to make money. The Boom-Boom Room was still there. Mama was trying to hang in there and keep it going as well and look out for the rest of us, but we were keeping an eye on her now, to make sure she didn't fall or something and hurt herself. Jumping the fence was out; I'd never do that again. One night, the house was full. The music drew people old and young. One of Pops' buddies came over with a twelve-gauge shotgun in one hand and a bottle of wine in the other. I was standing next to him when the gun went off and hit me in the leg, the injured one.

"Shit, my leg!" I cried.

Pops looked up to see who had the gun. It was one of his family members, who had a reputation for fighting, shooting, killing, using drugs, etc. Despite being family, he didn't mean a thing to Pops; he was just another guy. They started hollering at each other, and I thought someone would get shot, but they ironed it out, and the Boom-Boom

Room was back to business. As the night went on, the "victims" started to get drunk and sleepy. Before long they were out, and my brother and I started picking pockets, purses, and bras again. When dawn came, everyone woke up half-drunk—and broke. They needed a drink, but they needed money first. I was happy to offer to lend them some of their own money so they could buy a bottle and some cigarettes. These were pretty cheap at the time; a pack of cigarettes might cost you $0.50 and a bottle of whiskey would be about $1.50. I thought I was big stuff, working them for their own money.

We tried to clean up the house to make it look good. We were poor, but we adjusted to the lifestyle. On Saturday we had to wash Mama's clothes, using the rented ringer-type washing machine. Sometimes, when we didn't have the machine, we would use a rough board in the bathtub. We used these to clean the baby diapers. I had to wash them for the two youngest. As I mentioned before, one day, my younger sister was helping me out. We turned our back for a minute, and as she put a piece of clothing through the ringer, her arm got stuck, and her whole arm went through. We heard her hollering and looked up to see her arm it wasn't broken, thankfully. After washing the clothes, we would hang them to dry on a homemade clothesline.

One day my sister and Pops' stepdaughter got into it. My sister was not a fighter, but on this day she went into the house and came out with a handful of salt and pepper. We saw that she was about to throw it in her face, so we stopped her.

I remember my brother going to Job Corp to do something for himself. I myself wasn't thinking like this. I had this girl in my mind and had to keep an eye on things around the house; plus, we needed to move again because the house was in bad shape. We moved around the corner. It was much nicer, with three bedrooms and a fenced-in yard. I wasn't jumping fences anymore, but nothing could stop the Boom-Boom Room. That hustle was still on.

My second kid was born on March 26, 1972. We named him Junior.

One day, a recruiter came through the hood and asked if I wanted to join the National Guard. He gave me the rundown—first, there was boot camp and then you go to trade school to learn your MOS (military occupational specialty).

CHAPTER 8

Now I Just Turned 18

I was seventeen years old, but eighteen was right around the corner, and I was ready to sign up, so I did. The recruiter told me that he would buy me a fifth of whiskey for every five guys I got to sign up, so I ran through the neighborhood and got about twenty of my buddies to sign. October rolled around, and I was now good to go. We were awaiting orders to take our physical, which would be in about three months' time. Finally, the day came. I called the recruiter, and he told me to have everyone over at my house at 3:00 a.m. so he could take us to the VA for the physical. About eight guys showed up. Finally, he pulled up in a van. We all climbed in and completed the paperwork. The VA opened at 5:00 a.m., so we had to be there early. Plus, it was a thirty-minute ride, and there was sure to be a long line. The exam itself would last about an hour. In the back of my head, I thought I wasn't going to pass due to my leg injury, so I was relieved when I did pass. I really wanted to go, and I had put in a lot of work.

As I waited for the order to go to boot camp, I was just flowing in the hood, trying not to get into trouble. Finally, my orders came in. It was January 1973, and I was going to Fort Dix, New Jersey. I would fly into Philadelphia with a first-class ticket, a five-hour nonstop ride, touchdown East Coast, three thousand miles away from all the bullshit. It was a man's world, and I was determined to complete this mission.

After getting to the fort and the barracks, where I was processed, I got my combat gear, my shots, and a loan of $60.00 until payday, which was seven days away. This got you the things you needed for war, plus hygiene. After the seven days were up, you headed for boot camp—eight weeks of physical health as you got in shape. There, you got what you needed, and your life depended on it. There was a lot of walking, running, and obstacles that you needed to remember. In nine weeks, you would learn to be a man and a killer. I didn't complain, but there was a lot of work ahead.

I soon learned not to volunteer, because when I did, I was put on guard duty around the mess hall. It was about ten below and snowing, with a cold wind blowing. It was a hell of a blaster—I mean cold. On some nights you might be guarding something miles away from the barracks, on a dark, lonely road, but you got an M-16 with a full clip. There were general orders you needed to know, in case the wrong somebody walked up on you. He or she would have to be identified before passing you because that person could be a terrorist. You needed to stay focused because when that time came, you would be tested. If you needed to fight, that was no game. Some guys treated it like a joke.

The day of graduation, we all wore our class-A uniform, and we thought we were the shit. The drill sergeant called cadence, and we sounded off, competing against the other platoons. We weren't bad at all. Finally, we were young soldiers and men as well. We got our orders to go to our next duty station. They gave us two weeks' leave before we hit Fort Leonard Wood, MO. To start our training, 62B20 was my MOS, which meant heavy equipment mechanic.

My brother signed up as well and went to Fort Polk, Louisiana. He was gone when I came home, having gone to boot camp. We were both trying to do something for ourselves, because we were headed to a place where we didn't want to be.

CHAPTER 9

Mama Got Sicker and Sicker

I felt like I was somebody being in the military, and I was glad to see my mama because she was really sick. She didn't look good to me. That stroke took a lot out of her. Also, she was getting weaker and weaker. I just asked God to look over her. It was nice to be home, but I had to stay focused on the mission I was on by keeping a clear head and keeping out of harm's way. Plus, I had to deal with my so-called friends judging my woman. I knew I couldn't stop that; it was all part of the game.

The time soon came I had to leave. I took a couple of sleeping pills so I could sleep on the plane, but I looked loaded as a result, so the plane left me behind, as they didn't want any trouble. I had to catch the next plane, and I was afraid they would mark me down as AWOL, but they didn't. I was glad to get on that next plane. It was an American Airlines 747. I flew from LA to Dallas then changed planes. This time it was a single-engine that held only seven people (including me), 150 pounds of luggage, and the pilot. It was a short ride, about an hour. After we got there we traveled to the fort.

After I reported in, the fellows there laughed at me, but I was back on track, ready to start on my MOS training. We were in some barracks that hadn't been in use for some time, and we had to get them back in order—strip the floors, paint, mop, buff, put the beds back together, whatever else it took—then we settled in because the school didn't start for another week. It didn't take long to get together. There were about fifty of us. It was like school, going from one period to the next. You had to pass a test before you got your certificate to be a certified mechanic.

About three weeks into training, the sergeant called me into the office and told me my mother was sick. "Pack your shit. You're going home," he said. I took about ten days. The Red Cross put me on the plane, and at that time I didn't have to pay. I knew something was bad, and I expected the worst. I thought my brother would be there around the same time. When I got out of the car, I saw a lot of my buddies standing on the porch. *She's dead*, I said to myself, but she was in the General Hospital, in critical condition.

My brother and I got a ride to the hospital. When we saw her, she didn't look good at all. They had cut off all her hair and shot dye into her head. They found that she had yellow fever, which came from an infected mosquito. She used to go rabbit hunting with Pops, so we figured she got it that way. We stayed for a while, but she didn't know anything or anybody. She had lost a lot of weight. I held her hand and told her I loved her—we both did—then went home, knowing what lay ahead. I spent some time with my brothers and sisters, as well as my own kids. Time was passing, and I had to get back. When I did get back, I would be two weeks behind.

When I got back, they put me into another barracks with some guys that had been there before I left. A week passed and the next Friday we went to a bowling alley. I started drinking, and thoughts started spinning in my head. I was ready to go back home. I had $700.00 in the safe, so I went back to the barracks and called my first sergeant. I told him about the business, and he came down and gave me my money, then asked if I would be back Monday morning. I said yeah, knowing I wasn't going to be back Monday after a 2400-mile round-trip. I caught a cab to the bus station and bought a ticket, but I fell asleep. I woke up the next morning, and the bus was gone. What I should have done was go back to the fort. Naw, not me. I wanted to keep going.

When I got there, the kids' mama said, "What are you doing here?" I lied and told her they had given me a couple more weeks. She had a 1966 Pontiac station wagon at the time. One week passed, then two, three, four ...

Now I was AWOL from the army. Anything over thirty days and they would be looking for you. One night I was driving with my kids and their mama. As I drove through Jack-in-the-Box to place an order, some jerk hit my car. I jumped out to see what had happened and this dude got out, talking crazy. He was about 6' 5", damn near three hundred pounds, and drunk. I went to the trunk and got a bumper jack. By this time the police had pulled up. They got out of the car and started asking questions. The man's answers put him in jail. I said to myself, *Time for me to get back; there's nothing I can do for Mama now*, so I told the police that I was AWOL from the Army National Guard and I was ready to go back.

I was taken to jail. The next day they took me to a place they called the fort. I gave them all the information they needed, so they gave me a plane ticket and told me to catch the first thing headed that way. I went home, packed my bag, and said bye to everyone. I hated to leave, but I had to go. Mama was still in the hospital, so she was being taken care of. She wouldn't have recognized me if she had seen me anyway.

I got on the plane and made it to my destination. After I reported in, I had to pay for my disappearance. Then I was sent to the company commander. He socked it to me: forty-five days extra duty, sign in every hour on the hour and $300.00 off my pay. Yeah, that stupidity had cost me.

I got another call from back home. *Here I go again*, I thought. This time I knew the business. Mama was dead, so the Red Cross came and talked to me, then put me on a plane again. When I got there the yard was full. My brother had made it as well. We hugged each other with love. I saw my other two brothers and sisters with that look on their faces. It was sad for all of us. The funeral was held in September 1973. There were about ten of us, and we wore our class-A uniforms. There were six pallbearers, with two people walking behind and my brother and me in front. It was a nice ceremony and something I'd never forget. I wasn't a child anymore; I was a young man now, a young father in a man's world. Now that I had gotten past this, it was time to get back on track.

I still had to report to the National Guard unit in California and get a reissue. This program was a bit different; we had to go to a meeting once a month to go on the convoy.

Believe it or not, another kid was on the way, he was

born on the Fourth of July, 1974. He lived only ninety days because of pneumonia. It hurts to see one of your loved ones in a box, but he was in a better place. I named him, as I named all my kids.

The next month rolled around and it was time to go to a meeting, but we didn't go. We kind of fell off and stopped going altogether, but Uncle Sam won't let you get away that easily. We had to go back on active duty, this time for two years. Our orders were to go to Fort Orr, California, which was up north, about four hundred miles away. My kids and their mama moved in with my brothers and sisters as well. He was out on a hardship discharge so he could take care of my two other brothers and two sisters. My kids' mama would stay until she was eighteen then move out. My sister had a baby by my kid's mother brother. Afterward, she met another guy, got married, and had a daughter.

It was all right for a while because we were still in California, but I wished I had been stationed in another state because every weekend I would try to keep up and be a watchdog and do my dirt. Back at the fort, I was assigned to the motor pool as a mechanic. Each of us had a toolbox and about five trucks apiece to maintain. That was cool because we could keep up our own cars as well.

The first couple of days seemed okay, but after a while, it was straight army policy—"Yes, sir"/"No, sir," if you know what I mean. Now we were planning on getting a car. You needed one if you are going to be going to LA. One of my buddies caught the Greyhound home and came back with a new car. Now we were in business. We had transportation.

CHAPTER 10

In The Army

It was time to head that way. A six-hour, three-hundred-mile drive each way. This was our first drive, but it wasn't anything to a stepper. We were young and focused because this drive was perilous, particularly the part of the highway that we called the Grapevine—six lanes one way and six lanes the other, two hours long and a four-thousand-foot elevation. But you have to go with God because you'd need it. That's who I spoke to daily.

We made it safely. It would be nice to be home with the family from Friday to Sunday night, but that wasn't the case, because one Saturday rolled around, one of my buddies came by asking me to go to the store with him. I told the girl I'd be gone for a minute, but one minute became the whole night. When I got back to the house, yeah, she was hot, but she got over it. It was 1975 and she was pregnant again—number four this time. I was only twenty years old. I wasn't the father. I should have been. Anybody can make a baby.

I had to learn the hard way, and I did—I was challenging life and taking chances. I lived in a dorm with men of all colors. There were some white dudes there who liked to do

PCP. I had a partner in the hood who used to sell it, and I told him about my white buddies and that they liked it and wanted some. You sprinkled the angel dust over some bay leaves, which was the way we did it at the time. This time our car broke down, so we had to catch a Greyhound bus back. It was about a ten-hour ride. My buddy gave me about an ounce, and I put it in my laundry bag and took it with me on the bus. It was cool for about eight hours into the ride. Then it started to get warm on the bus. I had the bag over my head, and the chemicals started to smell through the bag. Eventually, the scent got to the driver. He spoke over the mic and told us to throw out the weed, or he was going to call the trooper, which was the California Highway Patrol. I thought he was going to call them, but he didn't. We were getting closer and closer. I had told one of the white boys to meet me when I got off the bus that Monday morning. Finally, we made it, pulling up to the fort at about 7:00 a.m. He was there, so I gave him the package and then went and got ready for the revelry, which was the eight o'clock count.

Lunchtime came, and I went over to their house. We sat down and split up about twenty-five packages for sale. I gave him one for his time, then got back to work at the motor pool. When I saw those guys, they were lit. I mean, fully. They had spread the word before I went to bed, and that shit was gone. I hope they didn't get caught. There were no cell phones at the time, and I needed to get word back to my partner and let him know it was all gone, and we needed some more. The closest phone was the company phone, which meant somebody would be monitoring incoming calls 24/7. I had a buddy who had CQ that day, and I asked him to let me use the phone, so he did. As I was talking, he was listening. He was an acting sergeant who was bucking for stripes. My associate told me where and when to pick up another package, so I had to meet another partner of mine about two hours' drive farther north from the fort.

After the talk, I went to the dorm and talked business with my partner with the car. I told him where we needed to go and he said okay. It was him and another friend of mine from LA. The car was a Pinto, which was a tiny car. Another dude wanted to come with us, but there wasn't enough room. That made him mad. We loaded up and headed out. It was about 8:00 p.m. I had to meet him at a shopping center. When I got there, he was waiting. We went to the spot to take care of business. After separating it, we put it in about twenty packages of aluminum foil, then placed it in a clear plastic bag and put it in the trunk of the car. We then started back to the fort.

As we drove back, the road was so dark I lost direction, so I pulled over and let the owner of the car drive. It was about 2:00 a.m. as we pulled into the back gate. There were about eight cars ahead of us, and the gates were closed, but then something strange happened—when the MPs saw the yellow Pinto, one of them told us to pull off to the side of the gate. He told us he was pulling us over because there wasn't any license plate on the front of the car.

Then he said, "I smell marijuana. Everybody out of the car!"

CHAPTER 11

MPS Open The Gates

We hadn't smoked anything, but the smell was probably in the upholstery. My buddy and I were put in the guard shack while they conducted the search, but before they searched he had to sign to search the car. When they got to the trunk, they came up with the bag.

Shit, I thought.

They jumped on the phone and called the boss—the CID (Central Investigation Division). When they arrived the first thing they asked was, "Where is John Doe?" meaning me. I was pulled from the guard shack and asked questions, mainly pertaining to where I had gotten it.

"Well, it's not mine," I said. "It must belong to you boys. I have no knowledge of it."

I was trying to figure out how these folks knew about me. My first thought was it must've been the dude at the dorm because we didn't let him ride with us.

"I know it's yours and I can't prove it," the inspector said. "When we catch you, you're going to be in the penitentiary for at least eight years."

Yeah, they had the whole fort on lockdown, waiting

for me. They took the dude who owned the car to jail and impounded the car. It was about 3:00 a.m. now, and we were about 4 miles from the dorm. Luckily, a five-ton truck pulled up through the gates, coming in from guard duty. They stopped and gave us a ride down this dark-lonely road. When we got to the dorm, I went straight to the dude and woke him up.

"Real tough," I said. "Why you tell these folks where I was going?" But he swore he knew nothing about it.

I went to bed with fighting words on my mind. *Maybe if I go to sleep, I'll have some better thoughts in the morning*, I thought. When morning came, things started to come together. If it wasn't that dude, it had to be the homeboy monitoring the phone. I was right.

The first thing the captain had to do was get O-Boy out of jail, like your parents picking you up from juvenile hall. That was military policy. After he got out, he had to see a lawyer. I had never seen a man in that state before. He cried like a newborn baby. I had never seen a man cry so hard and never shed a tear. He asked me what I was going to do if I was going to tell them it was mine. I said, "Man, you made that shit up. Do you think I'm going to tell them some shit like that? I'm telling you the same thing I told them: I know nothing."

Anyway, we had to go to the lawyer and talk this shit out. We ran it down for him, including how they can define the bag. He asked did you signed for them to search inside our car, and he said yes. Then he asked did you signed for the trunk to be searched, and he said no. "Stop there," the lawyer said. "We got a win."

The federal police were still talking about getting

the eight years if I was caught. They booked the dude for possession and drug trafficking but he was out waiting on a court-martial. When he got to court, there would be a general, a major, and a captain there. There would be a lawyer for the military and the lawyer for the defendant.

It was time to go. The prosecution made their case and we were called as witnesses. The case was dismissed due to illegal search and seizure. The dude was happier than a sissy in a frog factory, but he wasn't out of hot water yet, because he had to face the captain for getting in trouble. He hit him with an Article 15—a few dollars out of his paycheck and a couple of weeks' extra duty.

All I had to do was pump my brakes because all eyes were on me. Remember the lady I spoke about, the one my mother asked to look out for me if something ever happened to her? Anyway, I could call her anytime, from anywhere, whenever I needed her. She was like a second mother to me.

"Hello, how are you doing?" I asked when I called her.

She said she was fine and told me one of her sons had just got out of the penitentiary, which was about a two-hour drive headed south, toward LA. She gave me his phone number. He was only 4 miles from the fort. He was kicking it with an older white girl who was looking out for him while he was in the pen. I hadn't seen him for over fifteen years. I called him and we spoke. He told me where he was, so I went to see him. It wasn't far. I used to buy gas in that area. I had bought a 1965 Oldsmobile off of one of my army buddies (he's dead now). I had paid him only $75.00 for it, and it took that highway pretty damn good. Finally, we bumped heads. We chopped it up and talked about old times and a few other things. He had a 1965 Thunderbird and wanted

$250.00 for it. I wanted it, so he told me to test drive it and keep it for the weekend.

I wanted a drink, so I drove the car over to the PX (the army post exchange). Drinks were cheaper there, and there were no taxes or anything. As I was pulling up into the parking lot, I saw one of my partners from the hood. I asked, "What the hell are you doing here?"

"The army has a warrant out on me," he said. "After the police stopped me, I made a run for it. That's how I got here. They got me fenced in. But I got some freedom. I don't have to be back until seven o'clock this evening."

He rode with me to take the car back. As we were driving, he asked me when I was headed to LA. I said Friday. He asked me to pick him up and sneak him out of there. They were going to give him a dishonorable discharge anyway, so he didn't care. I said okay, so we rode to Seaside to drop off the car. It was a small town where he lived. After we got there, he jumped behind the steering wheel. We went whore hopping, trying to catch a nappy-headed woman, which wasn't hard. We headed downtown and there they were. One was standing on the corner as we got caught at the light. She bent over and asked for a ride, wanting to know what we were up to.

"You guys trying to get into something?" she said. "Can you O-Boys handle me?"

"Yeah," we said with a smile.

Now we were wondering where we could go. She said, "I got a spot we can go over there if you guys want to."

"Sure," I said. "Why not? That sounds good."

As we entered the apartment, it was like a kitchenette. Everything was in one room, but the bathroom had a door.

We were all sitting around when the party started. One thing led to another, and before I knew it, clothes started to come off. O-Girl was in her birthday suit. And my two buddies started to get a little aggressive, and she was getting a little scared, because they were manhandling her, telling her what to do. I was getting a little uncomfortable. I saw trouble. I spotted her purse and went in. There was $200.00 there. We were supposed to give her $60.00.

I came up with the money. "Look, I got some money," I said. "Let's get out of here." I knew she was scared, she started hollering, and I could see it in her eyes. They wanted her to do things she didn't want to do. At the mention of money, they stopped and looked at me. It was like winning the lottery. She was mad, but I believe she was relieved at the same time.

We hit the door so fast and ran down the stairs while she was in the hallway hollering in her birthday suit. Luckily nobody saw her or us. We jumped in the car and got the hell out of there. As I was counting the money, I said, "Shit, this whore ain't no joke. There's about $300.00 here."

I told O-Boy to drop us off at the base because it was time for us to go our separate ways. As we drove, we joked that this female likely had death on her mind.

The next day we roll in it around lunchtime. I was riding through town with my sergeant toward his house. I'll be damned, at the light, there was this broad again. This time she talked to the driver, asking the same thing. She got into the back seat, wanting a ride. She looked over at me and asked, "Do I know you?"

"No, why?" I said.

"Three dudes robbed me last night."

"For real?" I said. "I wouldn't do nothing like that to you, baby. I wouldn't need two other guys for that anyway."

"What you guys up to?" she asked.

"We're on duty at lunch. But have to be back by 1:00 p.m."

I was trying to get this chick out of the car. O-Dude didn't know it was me she was talking about. Finally, we got her to her destination and gave her the boot. I said, "Holler at you, baby."

As we were riding I told the sergeant that she wasn't been lying; it had been me and my two buddies. "The two of them scared the hell out of her and I was saving her ass. I thought she'd lied to me, but she didn't." He tripped out and started laughing.

"You have to watch what you do because you never know when you will cross a bridge again. That was a close call."

O-Boy wanted to get with that sister girl even after I told him not to do it, that she was trouble.

CHAPTER 12

Taking my friend to L.A.

Friday rolled around, and it was time to head to LA, so I picked up the car to see how it would drive. I got off work and picked up homeboy at about 5:30. I went through like a tornado, grabbing him and getting out of there. I had to drive all the way because I wouldn't trust him if he had a lap dance with five blind puppies. I just set my mind to it. Over the five-hour drive, my mind was on my kids and their mama. With about an hour to go, I hope everything's okay at the house.

Time wasn't on my side. The little time I had on Sunday, I couldn't drink, because I had to drive back a little earlier since the whole battalion had to go on a convoy for training. It was a long highway ride, about fifty trucks for six hours, carrying tanks, medical supplies, brides, ammunition, weapons, and all kinds of tools and heavy equipment, plus your sixty-pound backpack and M-16.

You had to share a tent, make a kitchenette each morning, and roll up your sleeping bag to keep out snakes and insects. We had fourteen days of combat training, including night firing, jumping in and out of holes, and tanks shooting at each other (with blanks of course), making you feel like you were at war. The weekend came and they let us get some beer. We sat around drinking and chopping it up. The sergeant got drunk, and he and I got into it. We made ourselves look like asses around the white boys. Plus, I beat him up. I hate that I did it; he was my boss and a brother.

The time was approaching to head back. The captain approached me and said that when we returned I shouldn't unpack; I had to report to the courthouse to see the district attorney. I asked why, but he didn't know. It was time to pack up and head back. Six hours is a very, very long convoy ride, but you get there. It was about 3:30 p.m., after a long, hot ride, as we were coming to the end. When we rolled through the back gates, the closer I got to the district attorney, the more I try to figure out what his business was. Once we got to the barracks, I peeled off my trunks. My buddy and I went for a shower then rolled off to the courthouse. I gave them my name then asked for the district attorney. He came out, and I asked what I was doing here. He replied by showing me a picture, asking if I knew this guy.

"Yeah," I said. "What's the problem?"

"How long have you known him?"

"About fifteen years," I said.

He said he needed a character witness. I asked why. My friend was in custody for rape, and he wanted me to tell the court what I knew about him. I said okay, and we returned to the post. I saw the first sergeant. He questioned me, and I told him I had to be back at 9:00 a.m. The next time I walked into the courtroom I looked around and saw that it was a jury trial. There was nothing in the room but old white folks. Now I really didn't know how this would turn out. I saw O-Boy sitting in the corner. He saw me and waved.

My name was called, and I approached the bench. They put a mic around my neck that was so strong, when I whispered, everything could be heard clearly. There were about six black people in the room. I didn't like that, because I didn't want to say the wrong thing.

The questions came at me. How and from where did I know him? What kind of person was he? I gave them a few details and left it on a good note. My mother and his mother were church women as well as friends. I had learned to respect the elderly and obey my parents. While in the military, I had also learned not to volunteer information, to speak only when spoken to. This kangaroo court was looking for information so they could hang this black man. Finally, I was taken off the stand. What a relief! I didn't know what the jury would decide, but I was done. I headed back to the base.

Two weeks after the case, I headed to LA to spend the weekend. I went over to his mother's house and ran down what happened. I asked her how much time they had given him, and she said three years in prison.

"But he won," I said.

She replied that after dropping the rape charge, they gave him time because of his background.

I had about four months left in the military until my discharge. My shoulder had been giving me problems ever since my training started in AIT. I remember hurting myself working on a heavy equipment truck. As I was working under the truck, I stood up without knowing that the door above me was open. The door caught my shoulder. When I went for X-rays, they found a problem—a chipped shoulder bone. Arthritis surgery needed to be done. December 1976 was my checkout date. The timing was perfect. I was admitted to the hospital in September, which left me three months to go. They were preparing for surgery the day following my admission. I went under, and then I woke up with an IV inserted in my arm, dizzy as hell, trying to understand what the nurse was saying. Finally, the doctor came into the recovery room to tell me that everything had gone well.

Payday rolled around the next week, and the lieutenant came in with his guard, carrying an M-16. The lieutenant was carrying a .45 automatic at his side. As I lay on the bed, I tried to salute, which is mandatory, but he said it was all right because of my injury. He gave me $900.00 in new $20.00 bills. I'd never had that much money at once. I was soaking it all in when the nurse came into the room. She burst my bubble by telling me I couldn't have this money in the room. I had to turn it in at the desk for safekeeping. I managed to keep about $200.00.

My strength was coming back as I walked to the PX. I bought about $150.00 worth of old-school albums—the O'Jays, Bootsy Collins, the Commodores, Cameo, and on and on. I got about twenty of them; you name it, I had it. Things were still cheap at the time.

It was time for my discharge from the hospital. The doctor gave me thirty days' leave. I had to wait until Friday to catch a ride because of my condition. After I got home, in the back of my head, I said, *Damn, it's play time.* There was nothing I could do but walk around the house and play good music and let the wound heal. I was just Cadillac-ing till it was time to get back. The four weeks went by so quickly.

CHAPTER 13

Discharge From Army

The day finally came: December 14, 1976. That day I was a free man—and broke. Everything that Uncle John didn't take, I spent going back and forth up and down the highway. All I did was play with my own mind. The only thing I got was a decent discharge. That's all I had to use to my advantage. I had to plan which way I was going next. First, I got my unemployment started in the army. I had a partner who is in the navy who gave me the ups on how to use my benefits by going to school. It was now 1977, and I was doing my best to stay on track. Finally, a few dollars hit the mailbox, and I went and bought me a 1969 Chrysler Newport. It was tan, with heated springs and pipes for better performance. Gas was only $0.27 a gallon at the time; plus, I was rolling with an 8-track. Low-riding was the thing, and there was a record I used to like, by the Commodores, called "Zoom."

Things were falling into place until I let that PCP get into my life. My buddy came from Germany, where his trade had been. He bought a 1968 Cadillac Eldorado. He and I were best of friends, but today he is dead. God bless his soul. We did some amazing things before I went down that road.

I've always loved going to concerts. During the summer I might go to the LA Coliseum or maybe the San Diego Jazz Festival or the Shrine Auditorium. On this day it was a concert at the Coliseum, featuring the O'Jays, Johnny Guitar, and the Isley Brothers. Everybody was on the grass, lounging and listening to the music. It was kind of warm, so I decided to go to the hot dog stand for a cold drink and a dog. I was standing with my back against the crowd, with my elbows on the stand. I heard some noise, and I turned to see people running toward me. This was the first time I had ever seen a stampede of people, running and hollering. It came to a halt right in front of me, so tight my elbows went through the windows of the stand. After everything died down, I found my way through the crowd, because this wasn't the place to be. I found out what it happened. This dude full of PCP was running around in his birthday suit, scaring the hell out of folks.

When summer came, that was the best part of the year. The Watts Festival was on for seven days and seven nights. It was so nice to look forward to each year, but it only lasted for four years due to lack of funding. It was fun while it lasted.

I was going to Community College in Compton, California. I was just faking it to get the money from my benefits. I had been slacking off and stopped going to school, so the VA stopped the checks until next semester hit. Then I had to catch up with the overpayment before I could get my check. My unemployment was running out, and the PCP was starting to affect me in a bad way. People didn't want to be around me and I was a danger to myself.

In 1978, I saved some money and went to Texas, where Pops was. I thought I could get a clear head, so I went to the airport and pay for my ticket. I dropped a bill, and it floated behind the counter. I looked through my money and realized it was a hundred I had dropped. I asked the lady to look for me, and she did, but she couldn't find it. The doors were closing, so they called the manager. The lady told him the problem, and he searched the ground. He came up with a $10.00 bill. He said this was all he had seen down there. I was in a losing situation and couldn't prove anything. They rushed me to the plane so I would be on time. I was mad as hell, but there was nothing I could do about it. I got on the plane with money on my mind, because my pocket was short due to the situation.

When I hit Texas, I had it in mind to stay just a few weeks, to clear my head of the PCP because it was doing me bad. It was cold; it was December, and Pops lived in South Dallas, living with the lady he had met (before and) after Mama died. I stayed with him but checked out the very next day. He put me to work helping put a motor in his 1964 Chevy. It was twenty-five degrees outside, I was already mad about the money, and now I was being put to work, helping to fix his car. This wasn't my business. My cousin's husband had a contract with a company to build houses and apartments after framing. There was a lot of debris that needed to be picked up. That was my job. Pops and Cuz would take me to the site in the morning and drop me off, telling me what to do. They would then leave for three or four hours, thinking I was going to clean up this cold-ass place, but I fooled them. When they came back, warm and drunk, I hadn't done any work. They were so mad they looked like they wanted to hit me. Pops always got like that around folks: talking loud as if he were Mr. Big Stuff. After I started speaking up for myself, things started changing a bit.

Friday came, and finally, I got a check. Pops wanted to go gamble, so we went to one of his buddies down the street, around the corner. When we got to the house, eight or nine dudes were standing around the dice table. Believe it or not, everyone had a pistol. I said to myself, *I hope nothing jumps off, because it's going to be like Al Capone and Pistol Pete up in here.* I'd never seen a gambling house like this.

There was a female there who was roughly my age. I zoomed in on her and introduced myself. We talked, and I learned that she liked to smoke weed, so we went to the back room. Before I knew it, Pops came in asking me for money, because he had lost all of his. "Damn, that was fast," I said, but I gave him $20. I couldn't let him know I had any more money because he would keep coming back for more, so I told him I'd left the rest at home. He got mad, and he wanted to pawn his gun, but they wouldn't take it. He was ready to go home, but I had bought some weed and wanted to smoke it. Anyway, the only thing I got that night was a phone number, but at least I didn't go home broke.

On the way home, Pops told me to stop at the gas station. He gave me one dollar to put in the tank. I went inside to pay, then came back and put $0.99 worth of gas in. As I sat to start the car, Pops looked at the pump. He told me to turn off the engine, jumped out of the car, went into the store, came back out, and threw the penny in the ashtray.

"Goddammit, don't let nobody take nothing from you."

"It's just a penny," I said.

"I don't give a damn," he said. "It's the principle."

One night, we went to a club. He was carrying a pistol, and that woman of his told him to give her the gun. He told her, "Hell, no." I never saw Pops listen to anybody, and that's a fact. He got that from his own daddy. Eventually, he did hand over the gun, but when he got out of the car he felt naked without it.

His whole family loved guns and weren't afraid to shoot. They were good people but dangerous. Pops had a cousin, and I was over at his house one night. He was playing with a .22 rifle. As his wife walked in the front door, he was aiming the gun in her direction. He shot a couple of times, right beside her head, laughing at the same time.

"Man, I said. What the hell are you doing? You could have killed her."

"I know what I'm doing. I'm that damn good. Don't tell your Pops. He's going to act like a damn fool."

"You right," I replied.

He had .22 pistol, and he asked me if I wanted to buy it. I did, and I asked how much. "Twenty bucks," he said. It was my second week here, and I was ready to head back west to LA because I was tired of this lifestyle already. For one thing, it was too cold. Also, I didn't really fit with Pops here sometimes. He was an asshole, acting funny.

Anyway, I bought the gun, and as the third week rolled around, I was trying to figure out how the hell to get it on the plane. What I did was wrap it in plastic and aluminum foil, put it under my clothes in my luggage, and head to the airport. There, I put it on the luggage conveyor and boarded the plane. At the time, airport security wasn't as strict, but I was still on pins and needles for the 1,500-mile trip. After we landed and went to baggage claim, waiting for my bag. Finally, they started coming down. I saw mine, and it was partly open. I had tied the lock together with two strings because it was broken. Once everyone had their bag, it was just mine, going around in a circle. I was scared. I thought everyone was looking at me. Finally, I found my nuts and ran over to pick it up, hoping nobody knew what was in the bag. As I ran out the door, I flagged a cab, jumped into the car as it was pulling off, turned and looked back and said, "Holla!"

I told the driver to stop at the liquor store because I needed a drink. He didn't know he had just helped me escape the penitentiary. That's where I was headed if the rabbit had the gun. I even bought the driver a bottle. We were drinking, talking, and laughing. I was trying to laugh off the danger, but I couldn't tell him about my mission. When I got to the house, some of my so-called friends asked where I had been. I said Texas. Some believed me, some didn't. Anyway, I ran outside, looking for my car, but it was gone; I figure it was repossessed, so now I had to start over. Luckily I still had checks coming in. That was the main reason I had to get back to LA, or those checks would have been in someone else's hands.

A couple of days after my return, there was a check in the mailbox for about two grand, so I went to the car lot and saw a 1970 Chevy Caprice. I asked how much they wanted for it. They wanted $1800.00 for the whole car or $50.00 a week. I told them I had $900.00 right now for a down payment, and he agreed. That car ran damn good.

I had a security guard job at night, with a nightstick and a uniform. I was working the graveyard shift one night, and at about 9:00 p.m. I decided to get a drink. I tried to get back before it was time to clock in, which was once every hour. I had no business leaving my post. I bought a bottle of wine and a can of beer. When I got back to the car, I opened the door, sat down, and cranked it. Just as I was pulling out, a car ran straight into me, hitting the front fender. Both cars were stuck together. They were trying to get out, two Mexicans reached through the window and hit me in the face couple of times. I had a knife on the console and was reaching for it, but everything had shifted, and I couldn't get it. Finally, I got out and looked at the car. There were about six Mexicans, all drunk. The odds were stacked against me. I was cussing these fools out, trying to figure out what to do, when suddenly about ten of my homeboys came out of the bushes. Now the show was about to start.

My quibbles done got big. I wanted that damn fool that hit me. My buddy and I went to the back of the car. He had a buck knife and gave it to me. As I was headed toward him, the police was at the corner. I had to pump my brakes because it wouldn't have been smart having it in my hand while talking to them. They stopped got out and asked me what happened. I replied that they had run into my car, drunk. The police were just looked at me and told me to take them to court. I tried to press charges but they didn't do anything. I was hotter than fish grease, cursing the police. They told me to be cool. My partner told me the same thing—just wait till the police were gone and we would get them.

We pulled the two cars apart. When the police left, we followed them home. They were driving a 1962 Chevy convertible. We sat parked where they couldn't see us. As they went in the house, I found an empty beer can, sucked some gas out of my tank, filled up again, and then poured the gas over the convertible, lit a match, threw it in the car, and ran off. The police had told me to take them to court. I did—I took their asses to court in flames.

We got the hell out of there, about five of us. We headed to the liquor store and I bought everyone a forty-ounce of Old English 800 beer and a bag of weed. I drove back to the house and parked in front, playing loud music. The police rolled up on us. "Damn, I said. They found out about the car." But that wasn't the case; they just wanted me to turn down the noise, which was no problem. "We're just having a nice time—that's all," I said. I didn't go back to work that night. I called and told my boss the business, and he said it was okay.

The next day rolled around and I had more luck than Carter had liver pills. In the parking lot, in the project were my brothers and sisters were staying, I was walking toward them, telling them about the previous night when I heard a shot. I turned to see this car rolling right into my car, and there was nothing I could do. The first shot came from the car, from a shotgun. As I walked over to see who the dude was shooting at, it was the Highway Patrol. He was on a motorcycle. He had laid the bike on the ground and was returning fire. There had been a robbery, and he was chasing the dude.

Bad luck hit and I missed my first car payment because I was sick. Channel 5 came out now and started asking me questions because I was the owner of the car. When I drove the car into the lot, the owner asked what had happened. I told him it was a long story and he wouldn't believe it but I needed another car. He gave me a Chrysler. It was a lemon that ran for a couple of weeks and then quit. Frustration setting in, I went back and told him what had happened and that I needed a replacement car. He gave me a straight bucket.

To top it all off, I had started doing crack. First time I saw a $10.00 piece and how small it was, I said, "I'll never pay that." I'll never say that again because, from the moment I took that first hit, I had as much luck as snakes got hips. My kids' mama started messing with my brother's wife brother. Now the odds were really against me—PCP and crack are a hell of a combination.

I finally shook PCP in 1980, but before I stopped, I was taking this dude home one night. He had a Sherman cigar dipped in PCP juice. He asked if he could light it. I was weak and said yeah. He hit it and passed it to me. By then, it was time for him to get out. I drove off, and as I stopped at a red light, the police were right behind me. I just sat there at the green light. Next thing I knew, the police were pulling me through the window.

CHAPTER 14

Police Beat Me Bad

It was a Highway Patrol, a couple of brand-new rookies—a white dude and a black dude. The car, gun uniform, the whole works was new. I called it on-the-job training. I believe I was their first bust. They took me to the sheriff substation. I was taken into this room to be booked. They sat me down, and as they were booking me in, one of the officers wanted me to pee in a cup. At the time I was very ignorant to the fact that if you refused, you got an automatic drunk-driving charge. I found out the hard way. When I told them no, one of them pinched my cheeks together. I yanked myself away, foolishly.

About eight of them jumped me. They put court chains on my ankles and two pairs of cuffs on my wrists. I was hogtied. Now I was on my knees, one cop behind me with his knee in my back, one spraying mace in my eyes, others stomping and kicking me. I felt myself fading out. They were killing me. I faked passing out, and they released me. I fell face first on the floor and didn't move. I heard everything they said. They thought they had killed me. They threw cold water below my belt to see if I was dead, and I moved, so they picked me up by the chains and walked me out, telling me, "We got your black ass now."

They drove me to the county jail. I was put on a gurney and went into the elevator, straight to the psych ward. I was put in a padded room, where I lay on a bunk on a 45-degree angle, my arms and legs both strapped down. I didn't open my eyes for about twelve hours; the pain from the mace kept them closed. The next morning they came in and still wanted some piss, and I told them they could get some. I was scared, and I couldn't take another ass whooping like that again, because the next one might kill me.

When it was time for court, I was put in a hospital gown with no shoes and put on the bus with about fifty other fools. Man, did I have a conversation about what had happened to me but I brushed it off, but they were clowning around, getting their laugh on, but I wasn't tripping. As I waited to be called into court, I looked down at my feet. They needed help. I had been barefooted the whole time in jail. So I went to the toilet and put my feet in the water. Man, it looked like a bowl of the yucky meat, HAHA!

Finally, I was called in to see the judge. As I walked over to sit down, I saw a few folks I knew sitting out there. Surely they were getting their laugh on. Yeah, I was looking bad, but the white folks don't care how you look or feel. Plus, they had me on suicide watch, which means they didn't let me out of their sight. The judge finally called my name. Now, I was thinking, how can I plead this case? I stood up and tried to talk, but he told me to be quiet. I kept talking, so he told his boys, "Get him out of here!" About four of them came at me.

I was removed from the courtroom until the next court

date. When I came back, they gave me ten months in county, but I was sent on to Ranch. I was booked in that night, and I couldn't see anyone until the next day. I had just left here about two weeks before. When the morning came, I went to chow, and I saw the fellas. Yeah, they got their clown on all right. The guys were fighting forest fires, so I signed up myself. It beats sitting inside the gates. At least I'd be making a dollar a day. They say oatmeal beats no meal. At the time I was going to school under my G.I. Bill, but the president at the time stopped that. I wasn't really tripping on the money.

When Sunday came around, my girl came to visit me. She snuck in a bag of weed, and after the visit I went back to the barracks and rolled up about twenty joints, each the size of a toothpick, selling them for $5.00 a piece. At the time you could carry money.

Ten months went by pretty quickly. It was time to go home again—hello, world! I know it wouldn't be peaches and cream because if it weren't for my bad luck, I wouldn't have any luck at all. After I got out, not much changed. I did leave PCP alone, but I went on to other things. I was starting to put pills in my veins, and heroine. Yeah, I was trying a lot of stuff then. One thing led to another. My brother kind of knew, because I wore a long-sleeved shirt all the time, even in the heat. I would tell him I didn't have any other shirt, but the family knew I was on drugs. It was now about 1980. I was out there homeless, with nowhere to live, going to jail for little shit, like public drunkenness.

I got tired of going for nothing, and now I started thinking about money again. I had a buddy I used to get high with. He came to me about a lick and said, "Do you want to do a burglary?" The people were supposed to have gone out of town. They were Mexican—how do you know that, I didn't know. I over heard them talking.

I asked, "Is it cool?" and he said yeah, but you never know how things will go when you're doing wrong. We had to wait until midnight for some reason. I said it was time to go, and we headed that way. When we got to the alley, it was really dark. We got to the house, and the back door was facing the alley. We knocked, and there was no answer. So what did I do? I kicked the door off the hinges. We went in, and the lights were off. The only thing we took was a funky stereo, a component set. Time was now of the essence, so we ran out the door. We knew the police weren't too far behind now.

We got to the dope man, but things didn't work out right. We were supposed to be about money now, but it was horse-trading. With our stolen merchandise in hand, we walk for what seemed like an hour, ducking and looking over our shoulders, trying to get to our destination. As we were walking, I happened to turn around and saw the police where they saw us before.

"Police," I told my buddy, we ducked off down the alley, and they drove right past us. We gave them a couple of minutes (a couple of minutes from the projects) and then finally hit the bricks. I asked him, "You sure this dude's gonna get this damn box?" and he said yeah, you could get pretty much anything from him. I wasn't looking for money. It seemed he would trade what we had for some funky pills.

However, when we saw him, he took one look at what we had and said, "Hell, no. I wouldn't take that shit if you gave it to me," then slammed the door in our face. Now we were stuck with this damn thing, not thinking the police were creeping up on us. We did see them once, on the same street we had seen them before. We kicked the box under a car, so they stopped. It was about 1:30 a.m. They told us to put our hands on the car so they could pat us down, and then one of them saw the box. The questions started coming: "Where did this come from?" I said I had no idea, but we were hot and sweaty and they figured something was up. After they pulled the box from under the car, they cuffed us and put us in the cruiser. As we were riding, something came over the scanner about a burglary. After about ten minutes, the scanner again announced that a house had been broken into, detailing what had been taken. The police stopped and pulled into an alley, got out, and opened the back door. My buddy was pulled out, and they told me to put my head between my legs and that I had better not come up for air or I'd be next. I heard a lot of grunting and moaning. Yeah, they were kicking that ass. Finally, they let up. Now it was my turn, and I had fear in my heart.

CHAPTER 15

Went to Jail

They threw him in the back seat and closed the door.
"Damn," I said, "here they come."

He opened the front door on the driver's side, got in, and sat down. I tripped out. He let me make it. As we sat there, I heard some noise, sounding like a tape recorder. I started to say something.

"Shut up, man. They got gadgets in here."

They were thinking we did it, and they were right on track. We were booked and charged with burglary with intent to commit larceny. This was my first case. I didn't know what larceny meant at the time. I later learned it means you'll do anything if anyone tries to hold or hurt you. When we got to court, the judge called out our names. We stood, and he read off the charges. I couldn't believe my eyes. He told the people who lived at the address to please stand. It was some Mexican people that we didn't know. He asked the question, but he couldn't speak English. There was someone there to speak for him, but he was breaking his finger pointing at that stereo, saying, "See, see?"

Yeah, our asses were blessed that night—that's for sure.

We should have been dead because people had been there and we didn't know it. God was on our side. If they had come out of that room to try to stop us, we would have done anything necessary to get out of there alive. That's how I learned what "larceny" meant.

Another court date was set, and we were sent up to a higher court, the Superior Court, which carries a lot of time. Now we were headed back to the county jail, on the bus. We had to come up with a plan because after we got back to the county, they would split us up so we couldn't talk to each other.

He asked me if I had ever been to the pen before, and I said no. He told me the sentence that burglary carries—two, four, and six years, not including larceny, which carries ten years alone. He told me that he was a three-time loser and if convicted he would get twenty-five to life. I knew I wasn't getting out, so he said to tell them that I had bought it from somebody and he was just trying to buy it from me. That meant they would drop the burglary charge and all I would get was receiving stolen property, which carried a 16-, 24-, or 36-month sentence. I pled guilty to receiving, so they sent me to prison on ninety days' observation to see how much time I deserved, not more than three years. Now I was at the county waiting on the chain to go to state prison, but my buddy got the case dropped (but he did do a 9-month violation).

I sat there about eighty days. During that time I talked to doctors as well as counselors about freedom or reduced time. Finally, my court date came up and I went back to the county jail. The first person I saw was my crime partner. We spoke for a minute, and he said, "Thanks, man. You saved my life." I said to myself, *And that will never happen again.*

We didn't know what they were going to do if the trial went to a jury. The lawyer came to me, talking to the DA about two years in the state penitentiary in the midterm. The alternative was to go to trial, and if I lost, it would be three years. "Bring it on," I said. I was tired of going back and forth and now I'm ready to get this shit over with now. I was in the system anyway.

Now I was headed back to Chino. This time, as I sat in the west yard, waiting to be placed somewhere in California, about three weeks rolled by. My name came up to go see the counselor, so I did. They had a spot for me, and it was at CRC, so I said okay. After the conversation was over, I walked out of the office, not thinking to ask where this place was. I asked the first person I saw where CRC was. They told me it stood for California Rehabilitation Center. Some people had to go there to do a program, but I just did the time. There were trades you could work on when you got there. I chose a mechanic. There were eight people in the class, eight men, and five women. Yes, there were females in the pen as well, but they were all up on the hill every morning. Five ladies would peel out of the van and come to a class, and we'd all be sitting in the same room together, the instructor telling us this and telling us that about the motor, the trans, whatever else pertaining to the car. After the lecture, he'd leave the room to go to his office upstairs.

You got contact with ladies here. You couldn't get any better than that. This dude and I had eyes on one chick, but he beat me to her. There was a restroom attached to the workshop, and so you can figure out the rest.

Overall this pen was pretty cool. You got a pay number that you carried around with you. It was funny money, but it was real money if you were married. Every other month you and your wife could spend the weekend together. I wore Stacy Adams shoes, street clothes, and Jheri curls. Oh yeah, I had a going on and made the best of it. I was paid $0.12 an hour. It wasn't any money, but oatmeal beats no meal. Plus, every forty-five days, I had a thirty-pound package coming in and $50.00 a month.

There were a couple of my buddies here from the hood. One was up for murder, doing five or seven years, and another had seven for the same thing. I won't share the details. I will say that he had a twin brother who used to be my partner who died of cancer (God bless). I was pretty much out there on my own. My kids' mama had kicked me to the curb. Now I was pillow to post.

It was about 1983, right before the twin died. Before his death, he came up with an idea about some work that was in Louisiana, something to do with shipping oil. He came up with a crazy plan about jumping a Southern Pacific train hobbling which was hitchhiking all the way. All we had was a fifth of Thunderbird, a piece of bread, a blanket, and a coat. It was a dangerous journey and a hard ride. Surviving was hard. For that ride, you had to be built like a piece of iron and have a lot of God in you. We got to El Paso after five days of riding. We needed money, and the only thing we could come up with was selling some blood. That was $30.00 a piece. Boy, that was a blessing. We hung out and finally got something to eat. It was a spot where a lot of guys like me were, hanging out under trees. They had a couple of gallons of red wine, a bag of beans, and a big pot. I guess they needed a cook. Well, guess who was handy. That's right—me. We blended in as if we had known these guys for years, talking shit and getting drunk. But the whole time we were thinking about this trip. We still had a few hundred miles to go, and we were really tired of this ride. We changed our minds, and the next day we headed back to LA.

It was a hot summer. We didn't leave until late that night, about nine o'clock. We jumped on the last train, the caboose. There was a couch, a refrigerator, and a radio signal. We heard everything that was going on, wondering why it was taking so long to move. Then, over the radio, we heard the conductor telling his boys to search every boxcar, all forty of them because he had seen somebody's foot getting on the train. Finally, they got to us. It was immigration police. When they came with their guns drawn, asking us if there were any Mexicans in here, we said no. They looked at us and told us to have a nice ride. We looked at each other and said thank you. We took advantage of the air-conditioning, the food, the whole works. The two days flew by, and we finally hit LA. It had been an eight-day ride, and this was the first time I was glad to see the county jail. We jumped right off behind it and tried to hurry up and get away.

After I got back to the hood, I was broke, thinking of money. One of my partners came up to me and said, "Let's go make some money." I asked how, and he showed me his pistol. He was driving a 1972 Cadillac. It ran pretty well for a getaway car.

CHAPTER 16

I started Robbing

On Friday night, we posted up at the liquor store, where people cashed their checks. We were sitting there, stalking a victim, when lo and behold, he walked out. As soon as he opened his car door and started to sit down, I ran up to him, putting a pistol in his side so he could feel the iron.

"Make this a robbery and not a murder," I told him.

After I got his wallet, I jumped into the car, and we dashed out of the parking lot to a safe spot. We counted the money. It was about $400.00. We had what we needed to buy drinks and dope and fill up the car with gas. We got high all night long and went through all the money. We headed to the liquor store at about 5:30 a.m., waiting for the store to open at 6:00 a.m. It was three of us. We didn't even have enough for a short dog (a short bottle of Thunderbird wine), so when we saw two Mexican dudes coming toward the store, I went up to them and asked if they wanted to buy some Mexican money I had on me (we called it funny money). Before I could finish asking, one of them cracked me in the jaw. I went down to my knees. It shocked the shit out of me. I stood up and beat the brakes off this fool. His partner started walking toward me with a knife in his hand. I didn't see it, but my partner got out of the car with his pistol and told him to drop it. I finished what I had started. I was doing him so badly his girlfriend was begging me to stop.

I told her, "You better get this crazy muthafucka before it is slow walking and sad music."

We all had shaken the spot because we didn't want to be here when he came back because it wasn't going to be nice. We went somewhere else to get our drinks. Later that morning, we saw this chick with my homie was messing with. She heard the story about me and him and thought we were Clyde and Clyde. She wanted to tag along. She had broken her ankle and was in a cast and on crutches. My buddy and I looked at each other and said, "Get in." We went to a county where there were a lot of shopping centers. She wanted to jack someone and there were two elderly white women cashing the checks. When she saw them, she jumped out of the car, put the pistol in their faces, and told them to give up their purses. Then she hopped her ass to the car, threw the purses in the back seat with me, and we jetted out. As we rode, I started to go through it, but she hollered at me to give her the purses. She went through them and couldn't find $0.30 between them. Man, I laughed for a while at that.

When we got back to the hood, we went to this grocery store. I was in the back seat behind the driver. There was a Chinese woman walking across the parking lot. She was on my side, so my buddy told me to get her. I jumped out of the car and put my hands on her. She hollered so loudly that she scared me. I let her go and jumped back in the car. We still had no money, so we headed back to where we bumped heads with those Mexicans. We were at the check-cashing place across the street from the liquor store, so we pulled into the parking lot, waiting on a victim, determined to get our money. As we sat there, a lot of cop cars passed us, traveling from the place where we had robbed the purses and heading down to the place where I had put my hands on that woman. I was thinking that this check-cashing place could pick up police frequencies and had seen the car the police were looking for. As I watched the streets, a cop car was driving slowly, looking at us.

My buddy cranked the car up and pulled across the street in front of the liquor store, and we parked as if we were going into the store. By this time, about twenty black-and-white Highway Patrol cars had pulled up, detectives and sheriffs and more. They had us pegged as outlaws. We were surrounded at gunpoint, with nowhere to go but down. My partner had a case pending on him and was out on bail. The detectives had him on a case we had done together a week ago but only he had gotten caught. They put us on the ground at gun point, including the girl wearing the cast on her leg. They searched the car for the gun but couldn't find it. We had to go back to where the robbery took place, which was Huntington Park. After we got there, we were placed in a cell. After a few minutes, the two old ladies came into ID sister girl, and sure enough, they did. They couldn't identify us, because they hadn't seen our faces. I had been in the back seat. We stayed in jail for about three days. Two sheriffs were standing outside the cell. When we stepped out, they told us we were under arrest for robbery.

We looked at each other and said, "What robbery?"

They cuffed us and drove us to the car, which was at the impound, to search for the gun. The fat-ass detective took us out of the car and had us look on as they searched for the gun. It was sitting on top of the radio, along with a snapped-off Cadillac hood ornament. When he saw the gun, he was happier than a sissy in a frog factory. He hollered with laughter and said, "We got you now!"

Well, they thought they had us, but all they had was circumstantial evidence because they couldn't put us at the crime, so they had to let us go. The girl who the ladies had pointed out was given an automatic seven years under California law—two for the pistol and five for the robbery.

Despite this incident, we didn't slow down one bit. In fact, our hearts got a little bigger. There was a grocery store across the street from the police station. We parked, and I got out of the car and walked through the parking lot, looking for a victim. I saw this white dude, putting an ice chest in his van. I walked up to him and asked him what time it was. As he looked at his watch, I pulled out my pistol and told him to un-ass his money. This crazy-ass white boy looked at me as if I was crazy.

"Hell, no," he said, and then he dropped his head and started running toward me. As he was coming, I was pulling the trigger. It was just snapping and snapping, but it didn't go off. Thank God it didn't, because I would have killed him. He ran head-down right into my midsection and we hit the ground, me on the bottom and him on the top. With very little time to win this battle, I went to work, hitting him in the face with the pistol. Blood jumped out of his face and nose, and soon it was all over me. Five or six seconds later he rolled off. I believe he broke his nose. I jumped up and took off running toward the car. It was every man for himself now. I ran down the middle of Central Boulevard until I saw an opening, in an apartment complex. I ran toward the alley and sat in a corner, scared as hell—if the police had seen me, I was a dead man. I had blood all over my shirt and gun. I heard a noise in the alley, so I got up to look and there was the police car, creeping along. An officer was walking at its side, his gun in the air, looking for me.

I tiptoed back to the corner and sat down again, praying. I heard some kids in the apartment next door and thought they had seen me, so I told myself to get out of there. I got up and walked to Central, looking for a clear path. I saw one and ran all the way to the hood, trying to sell this damn gun to anyone who would take it for $3.00. Finally, I made it to the hood. I saw my buddy-in-crime and I was glad to give him the gun. Now I need to go put myself in a hole somewhere because I was as hot as a forty-five.

This vacant lot where we used to play dominoes, drink, you name it. There was a motorhome there, and I stayed in it. I had a partner stay next to the lot. He was a little older than me and did drugs too. This family was staying across the street. There were about four of them, and they didn't like my crime buddy because he was messing with their sister. Plus, he'd had a fight with one of them and beat him up. They knew that he and I were always together. That didn't do me any good. As soon as I got to the hood, I saw the police over at their house. They took one of the brothers to jail. I had to leave camp for a minute because it was a bit too warm with all these damn police around, so I left and came back at about nine o'clock.

As I got closer to a lot, smoke was rising up from it. The motorhome was up in flames. After the firemen put it out, I went inside. There was a two-by-four up against the door, meant to lock me in. If I had been in there, I would have been dead meat. God had been on my side again. I had a good idea who did it—those damn fools across the street. The next day, a couple of my buddies and I scraped it out for a few pennies.

After a while I was getting tired of Watts, so I headed back to Compton to my godmother's house for a change of scenery for a minute and got some of the monkeys off my back. Finally, I got some peace of mind, but the hustle was still on. One of her sons had kids by two sisters, so I and he was pretty close and the same age. He died of cancer—God rest his soul. One day, his little brother and about eight of his buddies were sitting on the wall in front of the house, smoking PCP and drinking. He and I wanted some beer, so we took a walk and got three forty-ouncers of Old English. As we were walking back, we saw them still sitting up on the wall. We stopped for a minute, and then I said, "Man, let's go inside." We chopped it up until pretty late and then went upstairs and went to bed.

After a while, in a dead sleep, we were awoken by a lot of gunfire. I got up and looked out the window and saw two people on the ground. As I went downstairs, I saw this dude walking through the front door. He was limping and asking for water. I ran to the refrigerator and got a gallon of water and a cup. I poured him a drink, and as I was walking away, he hollered out, "Cuz, give me some more." I looked down and saw a lot of blood on his pant leg, so I told him to sit down and gave him the whole gallon. I went outside to the wall and looked over to see three youngsters lying there. When the ambulance arrived, they were all dead.

"Somebody else is in the house," I said. "He's hurt."

They cut his pant leg, and a piece of bone jumped out onto the floor as big as a cookie. I said to my buddy, "See what would have happened if we had stayed out there? We would have been on a slab too."

I moved over to another spot because clearly, it was too hot here. I went to where my in-laws were staying. On this street you could get anything that you want. You can get anything you wanted there, from crack to a nappy-headed woman and other things as well. The dopeman and his mother lived next door to each other on the street. He was the dope man. His game was so tight that he had his own clothing store. He got us suckers to do his dirty work for crack. He got about four guys and we rode around looking for this little S-10 truck. Once we found it, we popped the lock and then drove down to this clothing store. After finding a nice-sized brick, we threw through the window, shattering the glass and then scattering after grabbing an armful of clothes. For that, we got $50.00 worth of crack. Crack makes you do things you never thought you'd do—even things that might send you to the penitentiary or the graveyard. He told us to get rid of the truck, after picking it apart. What we couldn't sell we left for the police. We ended up doing this two or three times a week.

CHAPTER 17

Took ATM

Another time, we picked up a van. This time, the dude had a lick for an ATM. It was at a hotel. About four of us pulled in. There was a janitor wearing earplugs, so he couldn't hear anything. We put the machine on a dolly, and luckily he didn't hear us, so we loaded up and got the hell out of Dodge. Now that the easy part was over with, we had to get the thing open. It was late at night, and fortunately, we made it out of the white part of town. It was crazy, praying for God to get us home safely even though we knew that what we were doing was wrong. That's what addiction will make you do.

We got to a brother's house and picked apart the machine, down to the safe. We beat it and beat it until daylight, but it would not open. It was mechanic shop next door, and he opened at 8:00 a.m., so we went over and asked the dude if he would cut the safe open. We would pay for it, we said.

"Hell, yeah," he said, and so he did the job with a torch.

After it opened, there must've been fifteen drawers pressed tightly together. You can hardly tell that any money was in it. I looked and saw that about five drawers had money in them. We pulled it all out and couldn't believe it. There was only $5,000.00 there. We were upset after all that work. Turns out we had picked the wrong day. We thought they had filled it up but they didn't. We walked away with about $1,000.00 apiece. That was cool—oatmeal beats no meal—but we figured it should have held about $50,000.00.

We still had trouble, because we had water all over the house now. We needed to water down the safe to ensure the money didn't get burned. We needed to clean it all up before my partner's father got home.

I was smoking pretty tough at the time, taking chances with my life. Sometimes I felt like I was in a four-corner room without a floor. I mean, I was really a messy fool.

In 1987 I got a job at a naval shipyard undergoing a beautification process, which meant I had to pick up the paper and clean up the whole shipyard. I had just got out of the pen. I was back with my family now, and I saw they were in need of help. Being a groundskeeper is a lot of work, cleaning from A to Z. I was driving the company truck every day.

My kids' mama found a new apartment. My parole officer wanted me to come in his office every week to piss. When he'd leave the apartment, so would I. I did that for eight weeks, but it finally caught up to me on the ninth week. He was there with a booking slip. After telling me to sit down, two officers stood on each side of me. He gave me a bottle to fill up, and it was dirty, so his boys touched me on the shoulder and told me to stand up.

"You are under arrest," they said.

"For what?" I said, but I already knew, so he booked me and drove me straight to the county jail.

After thirty days, I got a letter from the board telling me I had to do nine months in prison—thirty days for every dirty.

Nine months later I was back at the house. Luckily, I got my job back. This time I got a female parole officer. I still had to fill up the bottle, but this time I put a twist on it: I bought a thermos that kept the water hot. I also bought myself a cigar in a metal tube. I had one of my kid's pee in the tube, so when she came, I went to the bathroom—alone, as she couldn't come in with me—and poured the pee in the bottle. I did this for about a year.

Now that I was off parole, I thought I was the shit. I started smoking like a broken stove. I even smoked the rent money. Once the eviction notice was handed out, I even started looking for another apartment. We found one right around these Bloods. I never liked the color red. I came up around Crips, and blue was my color, but I was never in the game. Anyway, I didn't think it was a good idea but had to think about my three kids. I had to get a hat over their heads. It was a one-bedroom, but we made it work until a three-bedroom upstairs became available. Now I was around these Bloods, which was nothing new to me. I knew how to mingle and get around that shit. Not only that, the street we were on was a crack city—and whatever else you want to. I didn't have to go far to get that shit now. One thing is for certain, you can't just run for it, so I just spread my wings. My kids were sixteen, fifteen, and ten years old. The girl was the oldest. The apartment was small, but we made it work. My kids were Crips, as that's what they came up around.

There was this brother that lived in the apartment next door, with a woman with two kids. He liked my daughter. Long story short, they got together, and now I have two grandkids.

After a while, they built an apartment across the street from us. When they finished it, it was filled up with Crips. One night, a Crip and a Blood got into it, and the Crip beat him up. The next day, my brother and I were upstairs in the house. I was using the restroom. The ring of gunfire made me jump. I walked to the living room, telling my brother it sounded like Vietnam. Somebody must've gotten shot. As I reached to open the door, my daughter ran in, telling us that someone she knew had been shot in the alley. She was screaming and hollering, "Daddy, Daddy, Mama is shot."

I went downstairs to see what had happened. She was pinned up against the wall. I asked if she was okay and she said, "No, I'm hurting all over." The ambulance came and cut her pants off. There was blood under her clothes and blood on her leg.

The Blood who had gotten beaten up had come back to retaliate. She was in the wrong place at the wrong time, walking through the alley as the dude was on the sidewalk. The shooter hadn't even known she was a woman until she turned around, but by then it was too late. She was wearing my blue coat and a pair of blue jeans. When he saw her, he cut loose, hitting her four times with his AK-47, two below the belt and two in her legs. Thankfully she lived, and she still lives today, although she is confined to a wheelchair. She was saved by God and her will to live.

When she was in the hospital, meningitis and spinal meningitis set in. The hospital told me to get there quickly because they had to do surgery. They couldn't wait. She made it through and was stable in ICU. She stayed in the hospital for 119 days. I was her nurse 24/7. I had to do the whole nine yards. The kids couldn't stand to look at the scars and the work that had been done on her.

Another incident happened around this time. My son got shot with a .22 in the shoulder. It hit the bone, but it went through. I was a father of six kids, but now I have only my two oldest girls and middle boy. My baby boy got shot seven times and died in 2004. He was twenty eight years old. Yes, I've had a hell of a life—a father at fifteen years old (and their mama was sixteen). The responsibility never hit me. We had to grow into it, the five of us. The girl was with her grandmother and the middle boy was with my mama by the time the last one was born. When we lived in the projects, the Jordan Downs, I had a son before him, but he died of pneumonia.

CHAPTER 18

Hit My Son And Hated It

One day, my middle son was out shooting dice with his buddies. I was headed to the store, so I told him to get off the ground, which he did. When I got back from the store, where he was again, back on his knees, so I checked him. Words went back and forth, so I hit them. It was wrong, I admit it. I thought I was right because I was his father, but I was wrong. He looked like he wanted to kill me, but I guess he knew the consequences that came with that. My parole officer was just around the corner. His auntie called and told him I was full of crack, jumping on my son. He called me and said, "Come in, we need to talk."

I didn't want to go, but I didn't like running from the white folks, so I went in about ten minutes before closing. I walked in and sat down, and he gave me the rundown about me pissing and just leaving all of a sudden. A couple of parole officers were standing behind me. One of them tapped me on the shoulder, telling me to put my hands behind my back.

"You're under arrest for assault of a child."

I lay in the county jail for a couple of months, waiting

on word for what they were going to do to me. Finally, I got word through the mail, telling me I'd spend eight months in prison. I refused their offer. Now I had to wait for a board hearing. When that they came, I had to go back to the county jail for the hearing. At the hearing, I was sentenced to four months, but I had to go back to the pen for that.

After I got out, there were a couple of months left on paper. The time came to get off paper, but that doesn't really mean you're off, because anything you do can be used against you to throw you back in. I was out for only eight months when I caught another case, this time for selling to the police. A young lady came through the hood. She stopped and hollered at me, saying she wanted some crack, so I went to one of my boys and told him to give me a piece. I was trying to hurry up and get back to the girl because I was trying to get at her. When I passed or the dope, she gave me a $20.00 bill. She was driving a black Mustang that had a baby seat in it, and I thought she was a smoker. After she gave me the money she spun off and hit the corner. Nine cars came around the corner after me. I went to this candy truck to buy a pack of Camel cigarettes to make a change so I wouldn't have any marked money on me. When I stepped away from the truck, they surrounded me. One cop jumped out and came over to me, telling me to put my hands behind me.

"You know you sold that dope to a police officer," he said.

They patted me down, and I didn't have any dope on me. I told them they couldn't do anything because I didn't have any marked money on me. They said it didn't matter because they had been recording at the station. We had been talking about it. If I didn't believe them, I could take my chances and go to trial, they said.

When I got to jail, they put me in a cell with about eight youngsters. We all got busted for the same thing. I was the oldest one in there, and it was filling up fast. I was there for about four days, waiting on the chain to go to the county jail. The day came to be transported. The police came and let us put on our shoes. One of the youngsters said, "School, you want some cocaine?"

"What?" I said.

He went on to say that he had some in his shoes and asked if I could sell it. He got it out to show it to me, then gave it to me. I went to the showers, so I shot it up the "backyard." At the same time, I heard them dragging the chain, so I had to hurry because if they caught me, I'll be dead. As soon as I buttoned my pants up, the door opened. I had to do what I had to do. I saw money signs because I knew I was going to the penitentiary. Plus, no one was going to see me or send me a dime on the bus headed to the county jail. In my mind, I said, *If they find this shit, I'm out of here. Bringing dope in the system while in for selling to the police—it won't be an early release.*

While waiting to get processed we were all sitting in a cell with about fifty hardheads, standing room only, all night long. The time came and they called forty of us into the shower. They made us get butt naked as they did their search. I thought *If they make us bend over and cough, I'm a dead man.* I got lucky. The shower wasn't working. They made us go and get sprayed for insect bugs. After that, we were sent for them to take blood. Now we were going to "Floor 5000," the fifth floor.

I got under an old-school brother. I needed someone to watch my back, and an older brother would do. He took me under his wing, and he had my back. When we got on the elevator, a trustee was already on it. There were about ten of us, as well as the police. Old-school was with me. He knew the trustee. They talked, and then I told him I had a crack on me. I told him where we were going and to meet us there. After getting off the elevator, we walked into this room with about 300 dudes waiting to get processed. As I waited for a cell, Old-school and I found a bunk. As we did so the trustee was looking for me, but Old-school stopped him short because he didn't want him talking to me. He wanted some of what I had, so I sold him $30.00 worth. He wanted more. He had $50.00, so I gave him $15.00 worth. Yeah, that's what you call jailhouse hustling. Had to go in and out of the backyard so many times to fish out that dope. A man doesn't like that lifestyle because it's not a good feeling, but I did it because I had to. Finally, I got through all the shit. I made about $800.00.

You couldn't carry around that much money at the time, but they eventually stopped that because people started getting lawyers and bail bonds. When you have that kind of money, you want to move it fast. I went to the chaplain and told him I had too much money on me, asking if he could put it on my books. He told me I shouldn't have that much money on me, that I was only supposed to have $40.00. That was the lick because I knew I was going to the pen. I was relieved—no money, no dope. The only thing I had to concentrate on was time.

I got settled in and lay down for about four months. Court finally came, and they came at me with two years in the pen. This was my second prison number. I took it and ran because I had nothing to fight with, so here I go again, back to Chino, waiting for my placement to come up on the board.

After about a month it said CCC. I asked some dude where that was, and he said it was about one thousand miles away from home, way up north. You had to go out of California through a city in Nevada, through all the pine trees on the Ponderosa Ranch. Yeah, that's right, where the TV series *Bonanza* was made. It was really nice going through there, smelling all that fresh pine. It took about two hours to get through and then back into California, headed toward the prison. The bus was well guarded. The driver had a pistol, and there was one in a front cage with a shotgun looking at you and another in a cage in the back, also with his eyes on you. Those guards were no joke. When they said no talking, that's what they meant. One dude believed his shit didn't stink. He got caught talking and one of the guards told the driver to pull over. The guard uncuffed him and dragged his ass off the bus. They beat the shit out of him to make an example of him to us. After that, you could hear a pin drop.

Finally, we made it, right after evening chow.

CHAPTER 19

Went to Prison

The guys in the yard so the bus heading in, so they ran up to the fence, waiting to see who would peel off that they knew—a friend or an enemy. Now that I was here, I just had to deal with. It wasn't that bad of a stay. After about fifteen months, the halfway house came up. Yeah, I went in when I shouldn't have. You had to stay ten days before they let you out, and you are supposed to be job hunting. Fortunately, I learned that my in-laws had a car wash, and that was the lick for me.

My ten days were up, so I hit the streets early that morning. When I got in the hood, it was the same old people hanging out on the corner in front of the store, waiting for a drink or anything else. I saw this chick that I had liked for years, but this dude she had a baby with had been messing with my kids' mama while I was in the war. We chop it up, and I talked her into going to a motel. I bought her about $15.00 worth of crack. The devil was trying to get me, but I went along with it because a guy was overdue. Anyway, we walked off and all eyes were on us. I didn't give a damn.

When we got to the motel, she hit that shit and then offered me some.

"Naw, Naw, baby. I got to go back with clear eyes," I said. "Can't mess up the first day."

We did what we did, and then I had to get up and get out of there. I went to my godmama to get the money she had saved for me. She was my heart, other than my mother—bless her soul. She was kind of pissed off at me because she knew I was going back. I was fooling myself by telling her I was going to do the right thing. She gave me the money, and now I had about $1,500. I was thinking I was shitting in high cotton, so I went to my buddy who had a 1976 short-booty Cadillac for sale. He wanted $500.00 for it, and I bought it. It was crazy because I had to park around the corner, since the halfway house wanted insurance papers and keys when they learned you had a car.

The next day rolled around, and I headed to the car wash. I got hired on the spot. Now I could get out every day if I was going to work or not. I started falling into my old ways. I'd pick up a beer, which was a trigger. I had a stopping point because I had to clean up with eye drops and mouthwash—the whole works.

Two or three weeks passed, and now I was getting comfortable. One evening I was riding through the hood when I saw O-Girl. She jumped in the car. *Here we go again*, I thought. I got a room, and I'll be damned if I didn't stay out all night, but this time I hit that damn pipe. I knew what the consequences would be the next day. I was feeling messed up inside, knowing there was a warrant out for me. The way back, I walked into the police station to turn myself in, but they told me there was no warrant. I went to the halfway house to see the parole officer. He was waiting for me with the booking slip. We sat and talked, and he asked me what had happened last night. I told him that lust had got the better of me.

He filled out his form, and when he was finished he put the cuffs on me and drove me to the county jail. I had to go back to CCC and do the rest of my time there, which was about ninety days. Another one thousand miles. Yeah, I was sick, but I did it myself. I pity the fool who thinks them folks won't lock your ass up. You got to pay to play.

When I got out, and with my kids' mama. I thought she and I were cool, but I had it twisted. When I walked in the house, there was nothing there but my clothes, and they were tied up sitting in the middle of the floor. I was now on my own. I went over to my godmother's. One of her sons had recently won a lawsuit because the police had beaten him up in his front yard. He liked PCP. Not that I'm judging him; my habit was even worse than his, and that's a fact. He had bought a car with cash, and a couple of days later he wrecked it. Within six months he had done it again.

He didn't really trust anybody but me. My kids' mama and his woman were sisters. Plus, we were the same age. Our birthdays were in the same month. I was about two weeks older. His mind wasn't where it should have been, but he was a good dude, and he gave money to help people out. He was my friend, and I miss him (may he rest in peace). My mind and his mind wasn't there where it should have been. He turned me on to a lady around the corner. I started staying with her. I sold the Cadillac to her sister for $400.00 and then I bought myself a 1976 Granada Ford. It had a cassette player. At the time they were using beepers and carrying those big telephones. My favorite girl was Anita Baker, and I had her on cassette.

I was still on paper, doing okay washing cars. The money was slow, but it beat no money. I started smoking again like a broken stove, hustling hard by any means necessary. If I really want something from you, you wouldn't know it. One day at the car wash, my boss (my in-law) came at me and asked if I want to make some money, so I asked what the business was. He showed me a $7,000 check with my name on it.

"Hell, <u>no</u>," I said. "I'm doing good. I'm not thinking about no penitentiary."

The next day he came at me again, telling me one of his boys had cashed one the night before. "Damn," I said. "I've been out eight months, still on paper. I got four months left." But I thought about the dude who cashed one last night, <u>and</u> I said okay.

I <u>made the move</u>. I would pretend to be an insurance salesman. My in-law told me what to say. About four o'clock that evening, I left to go cash the check in Long Beach. I was rolling, listening to my girl Anita Baker, planning what to do with my money. I drove into the parking lot with confidence. I thought this would all turn out all right. I walked in and gave the check to the teller, showing her my ID. She asked me how I wanted it, and I told her how to cut it up.

"Okay, I'll be right back," she said.

Five or six minutes rolled by before she came back, saying she'd need a few more minutes.

"Yes, ma'am," I said.

After I got to my car, I looked up to see two police cars

coming toward me. Next thing I knew, there were six cars. One of the officers jumped out. He told me to get out of my car and that I fit the description of a call he got. He told me to stay there until he got back and then went inside. When he came back out, he asked me where I had gotten the check.

I said that everything he needed to know was on this piece of paper, but still, he hooked me up. As we were walking toward their cruiser, I asked if I could lock up my car. He said no. He opened it himself and saw the papers I had from the county office's enrollment papers under the VA, papers on a slip-and-fall from a lawyer's office, unemployment papers, and so on. Yeah, I thought I had it going on.

"You're trying to make more money than me," one of the officers said, trying to make a joke out of it. It was no joke because now I was headed back to the pen. I was charged with attempted forgery. I thought about telling them who was behind it, but it wouldn't do me any good, so I waited it out. After court, I ended up with five years—two for the check and three for violation. They shot my ass back up there in the middle of winter, below zero. It wasn't that bad, though. I was thirty-five at the time, so I was moved to the old-man dorm. My partner from CRC was there too. I did about eighteen months.

CHAPTER 20

Got Out Then Got Cracked Out

I made a hustle around the house, I live in the back my brother lives in the front, with a little help from my brother, I sued the landlord for a few dollars, yes I was a hot mess. I was dealing with this female, she was nice-looking but don't pay the bills. We argued everyday when the dope, alcohol and cigarettes are gone, shes a damn fool. We fought like two gorillas in a wooden box.

One day we were on the bus, going back and forth. I knew where this is going, so we got off. I was walking away when she hit me, so I turned and hit her ass back. Somehow she came up with a knife, and before I knew it she hit me on my neck and on my cheek. I tried to break my foot in her ass—I wasn't the only one bleeding when it was over. I took the knife and threw it over the fence. Someone called the police, and the meat wagon came. I didn't want her to go to jail, so I didn't say anything. I went to the hospital and stayed there for about four hours before they cut me loose. It wasn't anything major.

I got home with tape around my neck. My brother and sister asked me questions, but I lied. Later on, they found out what had happened. They never liked O-Girl from that day on.

A couple of weeks went by, and we bumped heads again. She didn't have anywhere to stay, so I told her to come on by. I don't know why I was weak for this chick. She had a few dollars and so did I, so we got our smoke on. We were into it a couple of hours when the lights went off. That kind of spooked us because we were high as hell. I was just trying to figure this shit out when it dawned on me that my brother had cut off the lights. My lights were hooked up to his, so he had control. I told him to turn them back on, but he didn't, so I called the police. They came and I ran down the situation to them. They told him he would get a free ride if he didn't turn the lights back on, so he did, but he was madder than a boatload of tigers. He was so mad he would do little shit like put itching powder in the bed while I was gone. I wondered why we were itching so much, but I didn't find out why until later.

My family was still kind of mad at me about this woman. I couldn't get anything from them now. The best thing to do would be to dismiss her, because she didn't mean me any good, and I was no good for her. We weren't getting anywhere together. When I told her she had to go, she got mad. She slammed the door and broke the window, but at least she was gone and I had the house to myself.

The landlord came over to do some work—some old white dude, about 6 feet tall and 300 pounds. He liked me. He had three circular saws, a couple of drills, and a Sawzall. We worked until the end of the day, and he asked if he could leave the tools here until he got back. I said yeah, but three days went by and he hadn't returned. One of my partners came over with some crack. We smoked it, and soon we were broke. He looked over and saw those damn tools and asked whose they were. I told him.

"Hey, man, let's go to the pawn. We'll just take one and get it out tomorrow."

At first, I said no but then agreed to take just one. Soon after we took a second, and eventually they were all gone, about $600.00 worth altogether. Now I was thinking, what the hell was I going to tell this old white boy? He eventually came back to pick up the tools and asked where they were. I said somebody had stolen them while I was on the roof working. He wasn't buying that shit.

He said, "Tell me where they are and I'll buy them back." I again denied taking them, and he said, "If I find out you sold my tools, I'm going to kill you, nigga."

I didn't say a damn word. I got the eviction a month following the next day. This time it was the sheriff telling me I had three minutes to get my stuff out. I threw everything a couple of bags, and I got the hell out of there. The owner was there as well—a woman. I hadn't realized the old dude was her helper. She was mad as hell because I sued her and I had stopped paying rent.

With nowhere to go, I started cussing and throwing stuff. One of my in-laws let me rest my hat in the garage. At least now I had a spot. I was back in Blood territory, which was cool because I fit in—it didn't matter to me— but the hustle was a bit different. This dead-end street here had more dope than Carter had liver pills. It was a 24/7 spot. Folks got robbed, they got their carjacked—anything related to money, you were taking your chance when you came to this dead-end. Here, you lost respect for yourself and others, especially your loved ones. I had stolen from my own people. However, they never stopped loving me; they just hated what I did and what I was doing.

I was tired of this lifestyle. I talked to my sister. It was early 1996, and I told her I was thinking about going to Texas. About three months later we had the conversation again. In June my disability check would be in, and I was going to get a ticket. She thought it was lying. Well, she was right at the time, but when August came around, I jumped my ass on that Greyhound headed to Texas, with a fifth of whiskey and no dope. It was about a twenty-seven-hour ride.

Finally, we hit Texas, and we pulled into the bus station at about 4:30 <u>a.m.</u> As I stepped off the bus, I looked around. Finally, I spotted Pops and his buddy. After making introductions, I got my luggage into the car and headed to Waxahachie at his house. I said I would stay for about a year. Hopefully, I could remain drug-free. It was about a twenty-five-minute ride to his house. When we got there, it was dark. I couldn't see any sidewalk or streetlights. When I went in, it looked like the house from the *Munsters*—all dark and spooky, and you had to feel your way through.

CHAPTER 21

Went to Waxahachie, TX

Pops' wife, the one he was messing with while Mama was alive, said hi. I had to sleep. I kept the lights on all night. No TV. I put my things on the bed and went back into the living room. We sat for a minute. Finally, the sun came up, so I stepped out onto the porch, looking north, south, east, and west. I said to myself, *This is going to be a turnaround*.

I was ready to walk back to the Greyhound station, the way it looked down here. This wasn't the place for me. But it wasn't that easy. I was 1,300 miles away from the hood. This was deep-down country. Women were walking around smoking Black and Mild cigars. This town was *Texas*. I pronounce it the way it's spelled, but not the people down here.

The police courthouse downtown was only two minutes from the house. The town was so little, some of the people went to the same school as their parents. Everybody knew everybody. Some had babies by their own kin. I said I was going to stay for about a year. Hopefully, by then, my head would be back on track. Pops stayed on the corner. The town reminded me of the show *In the Heat of the Night*.

There were a whole lot of shotgun houses. My mother knew about this town Waxahachie, my mama also lives here and there were two old guys that knew her and two of my aunties as well. There were a couple of old dudes knew my mother and Annie's I couldn't believe it, but it was true.

I had come here to stop smoking crack, but the temptation was there, and the town swallowed my ass up but I did find myself a job working for $6.00 an hour. It wasn't much, but along with my disability was okay. I ran across this lady, and she didn't smoke—boy, was that a blessing.

Soon it was time to move out of Pops' house, so I and O-Girl hooked up and got married even though she knew what I was doing and I love her for that. She knew this lady. Because of her job is bailbondsman and the owner of about twenty houses she went out to try and help people in the neighborhood. She's deceased today and God bless her soul. She knew this lady who owned around twenty houses. Plus, she was a bail bondswoman. Yeah, that's right. She was the head negro in charge. She had the whole town sew up. One time, she got me out of jail on my word because of her job

I even rented a house. It was summer, and there was no air conditioning, so I had a big water fan in the window. You had to remember to put water in it every so often. That's something I'd never seen done.

I got myself a good job, working in a plant, cutting aluminum for doors and window frames. I was so good I got down to thirty seconds of an inch. I worked there for three years until a cut my finger off. I got laid off, but I bought myself a 1976 LTD. It ran well.

O-Girl and I got an apartment together, and she stuck beside me, even though I had gotten back into the crack and

I was an alcoholic. One night I got stopped by the police and was sent to jail for a DWI. That was number two. The first time I'd had to do 75 days, but this time it was 150. I could see now where this was going. My license was suspended. Now I couldn't drive, and I was put on probation for five years. *I can do this*, I thought. I had to piss three times a week. I had one of those by-the-book officers.

On Thursday, this dude wanted a piece of crack, but he didn't know what to get any. *Here I go ...*

"I know where some at."

I had been doing well for three weeks, but the devil tricked me. I took him and got it. He gave me about $5.00 worth of the stuff. I saved it until the next day, the Friday. I had to pee on Monday. I was so desperate to clean up I even took a teaspoon of bleach, thinking that might help. Monday morning came around, and I just knew that the bleach did the job. He gave me the bottle and we sat down to see what color it was going to be. It was dirty.

He was pissed off. "You're going to go to jail for two years, to a rehab penitentiary." I pleaded with him, not wanting to go to jail, and he agreed to six months. I was told to be there Tuesday and turn myself in.

I talked to the old lady, but there was nothing we could do about it. Now she'd have this whole house to herself.

He told me six months, but it took me fifteen months to get home, plus three months in the halfway house and seven in after-care. Also, there was $6,300 in fees, and it took twenty-two months before I got off the paper.

***

The turning point came in July 2007, I got caught up

Waxahachie, Texas. I was put on probation for five years I thought that was going to slow me down, but it didnt. They gave me fifteen months inside a rehabilitation prison. I said to myself this is it, I'm tired of being a dead horse, its getting me nowhere just killing my soul, after forty-five years I asked God to keep that taste out of my mouth and He did.

From 2007 until this date, I've been clean and sober—eleven years. I have grown into a better man, and I'm happy inside. I've had a tough life. I thought I'd never walk again. I believe I'll win because I never give up. It's been a long time coming, and I knew a change was going to come. Oh yes, it did.

I went through a program at the VA and I worked through it. I was what you call CWT. A CWT was a work program for addicts, homeless and etc, for veterans that's in need of help you had to check the boy every week for a UA. If you could come up without any dirty tests for a year, you got paid every two weeks. You know, I did a lot of ear hustling. I listened to what was positive and used it. I pretty much followed the "Serenity Prayer," God Almighty. It's nothing to brag about, but it's something I'll never forget.

I want to thank my brothers and sisters, and my two kids for not giving up on me.

I have accomplished a new home, a new car, after two hip replacements plus a shoulder as well. But I didn't give up and God is good all the time. I thank God for what he did and what he is doing. just don't take that first hit whatever it is! You win if you don't quit! I think about where I came from, and where I am today. I'm not where I want to be but I am not where I was. Don't be a me too fool.

Printed in the United States
By Bookmasters